SIX SALMON RIVERS
AND ANOTHER

Dawn on the Miramichi: Ian Bernard fishing a the Forks in the summer of 1972

SIX SALMON RIVERS
AND ANOTHER

GEORGE FREDERICK CLARKE

EDITED BY MARY BERNARD

CHAPEL STREET EDITIONS
WOODSTOCK, NEW BRUNSWICK

First Published in Great Britain by Herbert Jenkins Ltd.
3 Duke of York Street, London, S.W. 1
1960

Published in Canada by Brunswick Press Ltd., Fredericton, New Brunswick
1960
© George Frederick Clarke 1960
2nd printing 1962

3rd edition with revised text by Brunswick Press Ltd., Fredericton, New Brunswick
1972
© George Frederick Clarke 1972
Printed, Lithographed and Bound in Canada by Unipress Ltd., Fredericton, N.B.

4th edition by
Chapel Street Editions, Edited by Mary Bernard
© The Estate of George Frederick Clarke 2015

All rights reserved. No part of this publication may be reproduced, distributed, or transmitted in any form or by any means, including photocopying, recording, or other electronic or mechanical methods, without the prior written permission of the publisher and/or author, except in the case of brief quotations embodied in critical reviews and certain other noncommercial uses permitted by copyright law. For permission requests, write to the publisher at the address below.

Published by Chapel Street Editions
150 Chapel Street
Woodstock, NB Canada E7M 1H4
chapelstreeteditions@gmail.com

Library and Archives Canada Cataloguing in Publication

Clarke, George Frederick, 1883-1974, author
    Six salmon rivers and another / George Frederick Clarke ; edited by Mary Bernard. -- Fourth edition.

Previous edition published by: Fredericton, NB: Brunswick Press, 1972.
Includes bibliographical references and index.
ISBN 978-0-9936725-7-6 (paperback)

    1. Salmon fishing--New Brunswick. 2. Fishing--New Brunswick. 3. Rivers--New Brunswick. I. Bernard, Mary, 1941-, editor II. Title.

SH685.C53 2015   799.1'755   C2015-905649-7

Cover: George Frederick Clarke and guide, circa 1919.

Book design by Brendan Helmuth

ACKNOWLEDGMENTS

The author gratefully acknowledges the kindness of Harper and Brothers, New York, in allowing him to quote from "Penman's" article "The Restigouche", *Harper's New Monthly Magazine* for March 1868; the Macmillan Company of Canada, to quote two passages from

H. Blake's *A Fisherman's Creed*; J. M. Dent & Sons, Toronto, to quote from Charles Kingsley's *A Charm Of Birds*, Modern English Essays, Vol. I; W. W. McCormack, former Deputy Minister of the New Brunswick Department Lands and Mines for supplying him with a map of New Brunswick rivers; and Mr. Robert A. Tweedie and Mr. Fred Phillips, former Director and Deputy Director New Brunswick Travel Bureau, for their courtesy in reading the manuscript and supplying him with many of the photographs included in the book, as well as the colour transparency on the jacket. His thanks also to his granddaughter, Miss Mary Lord Bernard, for weeding out typographical and other errors in the manuscript; and to the late Dr. Louise Manny for her interest in the work.

PUBLISHER'S ACKNOWLEDGEMENTS

Chapel Street Editions gratefully acknowledges the enthusiastic support of Stuart Kinney for the George Frederick Clarke Project and his professional and personal assistance in bringing it to fruition.

In addition, we are grateful for the financial assistance provided by the following members of the Woodstock, New Brunswick community for the Project's book publication programme.

Stephen Thornton

Michael & Ann Campbell

Tann Papers

Stuart Kinney & Gloria Yachyshen

John & Lois Thompson

Publications of the George Frederick Clarke Project
— September 2015 —

- *The Last Romantic: The Life of George Frederick Clarke, Master Storyteller of New Brunswick* by Mary Bernard
- *The Ghost of Nackawick Portage: The Collected Short Stories of George Frederick Clarke* edited by Mary Bernard
- *Six Salmon Rivers and Another*, 4th edition by George Frederick Clarke, edited by Mary Bernard

Forthcoming publications will be listed at
www.chapelstreeteditions.com

For
STEPHEN AND IAN
BOTH
LOVERS OF LITTLE RIVERS

And to
MARY BERNARD
WHO
WHEN SHE WAS A WEE CHILD
DANCED ON THE LAWN
AND CHANTED STRANGE RUNES
(GOD KNOWS WHAT)
TO
THE FLOWERS HER GRANDMOTHER
HAD PLANTED WITH LOVING CARE

Editor's Dedication

TO MY
DEAR BROTHER
IAN BERNARD

CONTENTS

	Editor's Preface	i
	List of Illustrations	vii
I	By Way Of Preface	1
II	The Main Southwest Miramichi	11
III	The Way To Understanding	19
	Photographs—Part One	39
IV	The Miramichi Continued	49
V	The Saint John River	87
VI	The Restigouche And Kedgwick	123
VII	The Restigouche Continued	143
	Photographs—Part Two	169
VIII	The Tobique River	181
IX	The Upsalquitch	189
X	The Other River	201
	Index	203

EDITOR'S PREFACE

George Frederick Clarke started fishing the rivers and streams of New Brunswick as a child—trout for a few years, then salmon—and he fished them year in, year out, for more than seventy years. He was still fishing in his late seventies, when he wrote *Six Salmon Rivers—and Another*; he was still fishing in his early eighties, when he wrote another angling memoir, *The Song of the Reel*. He only stopped in his middle eighties, when bursitis got so bad that he found casting painful and prolonged standing impossible.

Writing *Six Salmon Rivers—and Another* was a new direction for GFC (as I call him here and in the notes: his full name is a mouthful). He had published ten books, but never before had he written about himself.
It was wonderfully liberating—"almost as good as having six vacations," he told Jane. He wrote in a loose, rambling, unbuttoned manner, a structure of no structure: about himself; about friends, guides and woodsmen; about his rivers and the sights and scents and sounds he had found along them. He told exciting stories about salmon he caught and salmon he lost. He told bits of the early history of the rivers. He told tales he had heard from woodsmen in canoes, in lodges, around campfires, and from his mother and grandfather: stories from the old nineteenth-century New Brunswick. They extend the reach of his narrative to encompass a century and a half: back to 1825 and the great Miramichi fire, which his grandfather saw as a

boy; to the 1840s, when his grandfather speared salmon on the Miramichi by torchlight; to the 1860s, when his mother fished for trout and helped her father tend his stake net; then forward from his 1880s childhood to the 1960s and the fight against the Mactaquac dam, with its disastrous effect on sixty miles of his beloved St John River.

Conservation

GFC's concern for conservation long antedated Mactaquac. In the 1920s he wrote against over-logging; by the 1950s he was seriously concerned about the rivers of New Brunswick. The Meduxnekeag Creek, where he fished as a child, was now so polluted that the fish in it were "unfit for food." He sat on an anti-pollution commission, but it had little effect on the policies of governments bent on building dams and attracting factories. He feared that the Atlantic salmon might be "doomed to extinction," in spite of the efforts of the Riparian Association.

The dust jacket of the first edition said:

> In 1638 rivers such as the Hudson and Connecticut were swarming with salmon. Today, due to pollution, all United States rivers from the Hudson to the Penobscot are barren of this noble fish. Dr Clarke hopes that the fine New Brunswick streams, about which he writes in this present book, will not suffer a like fate.

That was in 1960, when the St John, "this mighty river," still tumbled "with a song on its lips over the bars and around the heads of its myriad islands." He fought Mactaquac tooth and nail, but by the time he revised the book in 1972, the sixty most beautiful miles of his river were "a lifeless pond." It was a great defeat; his river had been "destroyed for all time." But he himself was not defeated. The dust jacket of the 1972 edition said:

> Dr Clarke fought the Mactaquac hydro project with both tongue and pen, and is determined, if he can prevent it, that our remaining rivers, streams and lakes, with their enchanting environment

Editor's Preface

that caused New Brunswick to be named "*The Picture Province*", shall not suffer the same tragic fate as the St John River.

Reception

GFC had a hard time finding a publisher for *Six Salmon Rivers*. They thought anglers wanted how-to books (how to cast and where; which fly to use), whereas GFC was alarmingly casual in his choice of flies ("What does a salmon prefer? After fifty years I have decided that it is the fly you fish with, be it whatever pattern you use") and distinctly short on how-to advice, except for one sterling maxim: if you want to catch salmon, keep your fly in the water. He was far more interested in telling stories—some about fishing, but some not—and evoking the atmosphere of his rivers and the camps and fishing lodges where he had spent many wonderful weeks and met many delightful people.

Would anglers want a book like that? Publisher after publisher didn't think so. In the end, to spread the risk, it was brought out jointly by the Brunswick Press and an English publisher.

It did not become a best-seller. Fishing books never do: the audience is too specialised. But it became a fishing best-seller. Hundreds of anglers wrote to him from England and Scotland, as well as from all over Canada and the States. Hundreds more sought him out in person. "Passing through Woodstock, which is a port of entry between Maine and New Brunswick, they make it their business to call on me and have a talk about angling." In the summer of 1964 twenty-nine anglers knocked on his door; in 1970— ten years after the publication of *Six Salmon Rivers*—fifty-two anglers did so. Over those ten years more than 300 anglers had called on him, and more than 450 had written to him.

It has never stopped. *Six Salmon Rivers* and its sequel, *The Song of the Reel*, keep being praised on internet angling sites. My brother still meets fellow anglers who revere GFC for capturing something they themselves have felt about salmon fishing: not just the sport, but everything they see, hear, smell, sense while they are on the rivers and in the woods: "yellow birches, hoary with age, some of their roots long since robbed of soil by successive spring freshets"; mattresses of "resinous-smelling fir boughs"; an owl floating over the river on silent wings; a porcupine waddling awkwardly; a deer whistling; a beaver striking the water "a smashing blow with its paddle-shape tail"; "the unimpassioned evergreens"; " the thud of the setting pole on the rocky bottom as a guide suddenly snubs the downward course of his canoe"—all of it "so interesting, so primitive, so remote from the usual haunts of men."

"A day off is a day gained," he said—a day off outdoors, preferably by a lake or river: somewhere that "renews and satisfies our spiritual hunger and helps us the better to face life with its numerous complexities: its joys and its sorrows." That is the overarching theme of *Six Salmon Rivers*: live fully, in the senses and in the spirit. Do not just glance at the beauty of the natural world; look at it, listen to it, give it your full attention.

The camp at the Forks, and the future

GFC loved all his rivers, but his favourites were the St John, by whose banks he was born and lived all his life, and the Miramichi, where he first fished for salmon, and where he and three friends bought the lease of a fishing camp in 1921, at the Forks of the north and south branches of the Main Southwest Miramichi, near Juniper. It had been a warden's camp. They repaired and enlarged it, adding extra bedrooms and a screened verandah overlooking the river. They fished there every year.

The camp was too close to the river; it got knocked by logs and ice floes in high freshets. By the late 1960s GFC was the only lessee still living. He was no longer fishing there, and the camp fell into neglect. High freshets had already taken off the extra bedrooms and the verandah; all that was left was the original camp, in danger of being knocked to pieces by the next high freshet. Its state distressed him, but he was too old to repair it himself, and didn't have the money for comprehensive repairs.

GFC took his children and grandchildren trout fishing when they were young. His daughters, Jane and Dees, fished a bit, but didn't become anglers. Nor did I, his granddaughter, though he took me fishing in Lane's Creek, above Woodstock, one summer dawn when I was four, and I still remember the excitement of catching my first—and last—trout, and how delicious it was fried for breakfast.

But his grandsons Ian and Stephen became anglers, and Ian has remained serious about salmon fishing. He loved, and loves, fishing at the Forks and in nearby pools, and now holds the lease of the camp. Through the 1970s and 1980s he kept it in repair, and in 1992 he had it completely rebuilt, adhering as closely as possible to the plan of the camp in the early 1920s, with one important exception. To make it safer during freshets, he had the new camp moved back ten feet and raised six feet onto new and more robust underpinnings. He named the new camp for GFC's second fishing memoir: over the door hangs a sign with the words, "Song of the Reel." Like his grandfather, Ian fishes at the Forks every year. GFC would be happy to know that; happy to see the shipshape new-built camp; even happier to see the sign over the door—and happiest of all that Chapel Street Editions and the George Frederick Clarke Project are bringing his fishing memoirs to new generations of readers and anglers.

Text

This is the fourth edition of *Six Salmon Rivers*. I have based it on the third edition of 1972, which GFC revised. I have silently corrected a few typos.

I have kept GFC's footnotes, numbered A-H. I have added footnotes, numbered 1-45, giving sources for quotations that GFC left unattributed, a few dates, and definitions for words that may have become obscure in the fifty-five years since the first edition.

Illustrations

The illustrations in earlier editions of *Six Salmon Rivers* were mostly of anonymous fishermen. I have never found them interesting, and in this edition I use instead photographs of GFC the fisherman, his rivers, his fishing friends and his guides. Most of them illustrate specific passages, and I have given the number of the illustration in parentheses in the text. In a few cases the correspondence between text and illustration is very loose.

There are, for instance, no photographs of GFC fishing as a child, so I have included photographs of his young daughters fishing.

The last page of illustrations includes a map of New Brunswick showing the six salmon rivers.

About myself and the GFC Project

I am Jane's daughter; GFC was my grandfather.

Chapel Street Editions has undertaken a publishing project which it calls the George Frederick Clarke Project. Three books launch the Project:

- my biography of GFC, *The Last Romantic: George Frederick Clarke, Master Storyteller of New Brunswick*
- GFC's fishing memoir *Six Salmon Rivers—and Another*
- GFC's wonderful short stories, *The Ghost of Nackawick Portage: the Collected Short Stories of George Frederick Clarke.*

GFC's complete works will come out over the next few years.

Acknowledgments

I want to thank Ian Bernard for answering my many questions about angling. My deepest thanks are due to Keith Helmuth, who conceived the George Frederick Clarke project and is making it all happen.

Mary Bernard
Cambridge, England,
June 2015

LIST OF ILLUSTRATIONS

Initials in parentheses are those of the photographer:
GFC George Frederick Clarke
MLB Mary Lord Bernard
Photo credits follow the list of illustrations.

Ian Bernard fishing at the Forks in the summer of 1972
(MLB) *Frontispiece*

1. a) GFC's grandfather Moses Harris, c. 1907
   b) GFC's mother, Maria Harris Clarke, about 15 years old, c. 1866
   c) GFC's young daughter Dees fishing at Taffa Lake, c. 1924
   d) GFC's young daughter Jane with a trout at the Forks, c. 1919-1920

2. a) GFC and friends camping with rods and guns, c. 1902
   b) GFC and five friends on fishing trip to Jackson's Falls, 1904
   c) GFC and two friends with trout, Jackson's Falls, 1904

3. a) GFC with trout, c. 1909
   b) The St John River above Woodstock, summer 1964 *(MLB)*
   c) GFC on the ice, with trout and snowshoes, c. 1909
   d) Men fishing the Hartland pool, 1950s
   e) The St John River north of Hartland, summer 1967 *(MLB)*

4   Two weeks at the Forks of the Main Southwest Miramichi, June 1916
    a) Murdoch Mackenzie, Henry Wilson, GFC, Ruby Clarke and friend
    b) Henry Wilson and GFC with trout

5   GFC with trout, Miramichi, June 27 1916

6. GFC fishing for salmon at the Forks, c. 1916
    a) Waiting for a rise
    b) Netting a salmon

7   a) The Forks of the Miramichi, looking upriver, 1971
    b) Jane, Dees and Murdoch Mackenzie at the Forks, c. 1925
    c) The Forks in 1997 *(MLB)*

8. Fisherwoman and guide, drawing by H.E.M. Sellen, 1931

9. a) GFC holding two salmon, early 1920s
    b) Anglers and guides, GFC and Noel Moulton in the lead canoe
    c) Dr Grant holding two salmon, 1920s
    d) GFC, Bill Kennedy and Charlie Clark, probably October 1948

10. GFC holding a salmon, probably on the Miramichi, c. 1924

11. a) Russell Boyer and Angus Bernard at Russell's camp, c. 1944
    b) Jane Bernard preparing food at Russell's camp, c. 1944

12. Russell Boyer poling his canoe

13. GFC holding a 28-lb. salmon on the Kedgwick, 1925

14. Guy Ferguson gaffing a salmon, c. 1925 *(GFC)*

List of Illustrations

15. a) and b) Anglers and guides, including GFC, 1930s

16. Jock Ogilvy poling on the Restigouche

17. "The Million-Dollar View" Narrows, Tobique River, before 1951

18. GFC with two days' catch, Gulquac Lodge, Tobique River, May 26th 1927

18. a) Noel Bear smoking meat, painting by Tappan Adney, c. 1893
    b) Tom Moulton, c. 1890-1910
    c) Map of New Brunswick showing the six salmon rivers

Sources of Illustrations

Plates 4a-b, 6b, 9a and 15b: Stephen Homer collection.
Plate 7a: Archaeological Research Laboratory, Department of Anthropology, University of New Brunswick, Fredericton.
Plate 19a: courtesy of Frank Creighton.
All other illustrations are from the editor's collection.
I have digitally edited and restored all photographs and illustrations.

— CHAPTER I —

BY WAY OF PREFACE

    Most events in my early childhood have faded from memory; a few stand out as though they had happened only yesterday. In particular the day when—four years old—and fed up with being dressed in kilts, I donned my older brother's trousers. The legs were too long by a foot, so I rolled them above my knees, marched downstairs, and announced to my mother that never more would I wear girls' clothes. I didn't. She went to town and purchased for me a pair of knickerbockers. I was the happiest boy in Woodstock. Later, when I learned that one of my Highland ancestors had served in the famous Black Watch on many a battlefield, I would have gladly worn the kilt. That dignity was reserved for a younger brother.

    Following a short period of which I remember nothing, emerge other unforgettable happenings. Our home was on a high, level bench on the north side of the Gully, which debouches from the Meduxnekeag River—called the Creek. It was late afternoon. Standing in front of the house—facing the Gully—I saw a man, seated in a small boat, dropping something into the water. I ran to my mother, who was planting flower seeds in the garden, and told her what I had seen. She informed me the man was Duffy Brawn, and he was setting a net in which to catch fish.

    The next morning he appeared on the path, that led from the Gully past our house, carrying a half-bushel basket almost filled with fish. Coming to where I stood, he lowered the basket for me to see his catch. I gazed at them with awe and admiration. All I could say was "Oh!—Oh!"

He gave a low laugh. "Want one?" he asked.

I nodded happily, and he said: "Well, take your pick, Sonny."

Among the fish were several trout, although I didn't then know them as such, and their carmine and golden spots—as golden as the marigolds that flourished in our garden—fascinated me. "I'd like that one," I said, pointing to a beauty that would weigh a pound and a half. Then, realizing that perhaps I had taken an unfair advantage of his liberality, I added, "Or that," indicating one half the size of my former choice.

Then the big man gave a slow smile and, quite as though he knew the heart of a small boy, lifted out the big trout and put it into my eager hands. "There," he said, "take it to your mother, and tell her to cook it for your dinner."

I was so thrilled, so overcome by his generosity, that I could barely murmur my thanks. He said: "You're welcome, Sonny," picked up his basket and departed. Thereafter Duffy Brawn was one of my heroes.

My mother cleaned the trout, rolled it in cornmeal, fried it in butter, and we had it for dinner.

* * *

Who that has eaten trout, fresh from the water, will ever forget the occasion? Personally I prefer small trout—eight or ten inches. And the best place to cook them is beside a meandering brook tinkling over its rocky bed, with wild flowers, and alders along its banks, and slender white birches, like tall tapers, set against a background of evergreens, and yellow birches, hoary with age, some of their roots long since robbed of soil by successive spring freshets. Perhaps you who read this will remember the fallen log where the brook steals from the woods and glides through the pasture. The log lies at an angle, backs up the water making quite a deep pool. And near the bank fleecy-white foam had lodged. You remember, perhaps, the day you first discovered it, and, dropping your baited hook just above the foam, let it float down and beneath it. There was a sudden, sharp tug at your line; the alder

By Way Of Preface

pole bent almost double; you struck and flung to shore among the ferns and bushes a ten-inch trout.*(1c-d)* And after you had killed it with a merciful blow over the head, you again waded into the brook, again dropped your bait near the huge pan of foam. Possibly you landed half a dozen beauties from this magic pool, stringing them on a forked alder branch you cut and trimmed with your jack-knife. No fancy creel of wicker or basket-ash for you at this early date. You were using what primitive man did thousands of years ago; and what every boy, who has fished, has used.*(2a-c)*

Every boy remembers his favourite brook. It is the brook in which he first fished and had good luck. I have fished the most famous trout and salmon streams in the world, and landed fish thirty times the weight of my largest trout caught in a brook, but, looking backward over the years, I find that my most enchanting fishing experiences were those of my childhood when, wet to the middle, I tiredly slogged home with my string of brook trout and received my Mother's: "Well done! You do know how to catch them."*(3a/c)*

As I write this I am thinking of Lord Beaverbrook—New Brunswick's greatest benefactor—who as a lad named Max Aitken lived in the old Presbyterian Manse at Newcastle, and used to go with his parents, brothers and sisters, to a cottage at Beaver Brook. Of course the title he chose when made a peer was in commemoration of this happy retreat, but I also like to think that he often fished the brook and took from it many fat trout.

* * *

My very first attempt to catch fish was in late March following my fifth birthday. The previous night a heavy fall of snow had covered the roof of our house and added its quota to that already on the ground. By midday that on the roof had rapidly melted under the hot rays of the sun, and formed little puddles in the snow below the wide eaves. Here was water. Fish lived in water. I broached my longing to my mother. She got a piece of twine string, fastened one end to a bent pin, and the other to a short length of cedar wood such as we used for starting the fire in the kitchen stove. Then she thrust a morsel of cold meat over the pinhook and with a gentle smile handed me my outfit. Going outdoors I dropped my bait in one of the puddles and waited for a bite. Carefully, with patience and faith that would have won the approval of dear old Izaak Walton,[1] I tried every puddle the whole length of the eaves. My boots absorbed the snow water and my feet got cold. But I cared not; I was fishing; and when a couple of hours later my mother called me in to supper I confidently told myself that, although I had caught no fish today, they must certainly occupy the pools on the morrow. But alas! It rained that night—a warm rain that carried away all the snow and with it the puddles I had so ardently fished.

* * *

Then there is the enchanting recollection of stories my mother told me about pioneer life along the Main Southwest Miramichi River where she had been born, grown to womanhood, married my father, and whence, five years after, she moved with him to Woodstock.

One story especially captivated me and was food for my imagination—which has always been active. It happened that, one afternoon, about the year 1838,[2] my grandfather decided to pole his pine dugout canoe seven miles to the village of Blackville for some needed supplies, and grandmother expressed the desire to go with him. Their first child, a boy, was then only eight months old, so he was carried to the shore in his small wooden cradle, which was set in the middle of the canoe. Then my grandmother got in, and once she was seated, grandfather followed, picked up his setting pole, and began poling up the swift current.

It was late in the evening before they had finished shopping and visiting, and begun the return journey to White Rapids. Before long, darkness settled over the river and the surrounding hills. Then grandfather drew in to shore and filled an iron basket—called a noggin—with pitch-pine which he lighted, and suspended it on an iron crane over the bow of the canoe.

---

1 1594-1683, author of *The Compleat Angler*, first published in 1653.

2 Probably 1845. GFC's dates are often impressionistic. Moses Harris and Johannah Curtis were married on June 11, 1844. Their eldest son was baptised on 20 March 1845.

By Way Of Preface

Grandmother took his place in the stern, and guided the craft down the river, while he stood upright in the bow, back of the flare, his long-handled salmon spear poised for action.*(1a)*

The flambeau cast its golden circle over the water, which was alive with a late run of salmon on their way to the spawning bars on the upper reaches of the river. The light attracted rather than alarmed them. For an expert such as my grandfather it was a quite simple task to take them one after another, throwing them behind him in the bottom of the canoe. He speared fifty great salmon that night, and only stopped taking more at my grandmother's stern command after one of the fish rolled over into the cradle and awakened the sleeping baby.

Yes—the Miramichi was a great salmon river six-score years ago. Often the settlers took so many during the spring, summer, and autumn runs, that some were used to fertilize the land. It is still a great salmon river.

* * *

My mother told me that once she and her older sister spent all of one night on the beach with their father near his stake net; and every hour, or sooner, they had to empty it, else the heavy run of fish would have carried it away or broken the mesh.*(1b)* She said they made a little fire of driftwood and sat beside it. Just as day was dawning a big bull moose scrambled down the bank a few rods distant, plunged into the river and swam to the opposite shore. How I loved that story. In those far days all the settlers had stake nets, drifted for salmon, or speared them; sometimes all three. And at the mouth of the brook that ran through grandfather's farm an angler, with a hook baited with a piece of pork or venison, could take innumerable sea trout, some weighing as much as five pounds, during the early June run. As for herring and gaspereau, and smelts. One could stand on the shore with a long-handled dip-net and fill a barrel in an hour.

Such tales as these my mother told me, and I never tired of hearing them. Both she and my father always referred to their birthplace as *home*. A vacation meant *going over home*, and thus it was as long as they lived.

Six Salmon Rivers and Another

* * *

The Meduxnekeag River separates the north and south portions of the town of Woodstock and vents into the Saint John River. It was once a famous stream for salmon, but for many years a concrete dam has obstructed passage to their old spawning beds; and only a few in early spring—when the main river backs up—are now able to make the leap. Moreover, the Meduxnekeag is filled with sewage from the neighbouring town of Houlton, in the State of Maine, as well with potato residue sluiced into the stream from several starch factories. But it is one of the finest trout streams I know, sea trout ascending it in the early spring from the Saint John. Fifty-five years ago—one August afternoon—I landed eight.[3] I cleaned and put them for the night in a cold spring brook; the following day I returned to town and set the basket containing them on the scales in a grocery store. Basket and fish weighed twenty-one pounds. The largest fish, weighed separately, went four and one quarter pounds. Yet today the fish taken from this stream are unfit for food. What a pity! Once the Meduxnekeag was "water which a Pagan would have worshipped in its purity, and we worship only with pollution."[4]

I have been told that a hundred years ago the Indians went up the Meduxnekeag and speared the pools, coming down in the mornings with their canoes half filled with salmon, which they smoked on wooden racks at the stream's mouth.

When I was nine years of age many salmon were taken on the fly in the basin—just below the wooden dam that had been built to divert a flow of water to run a grist mill. Several times after school I had watched anglers playing fish and landing them; so one Saturday I decided to try my luck. I had cut a long supple spruce pole, peeled off the bark, and from my father's store got about thirty-five feet of strong white cord. One end I tied about the butt and ran the remainder to the tip about which I carefully wound it.

I found that several men were fishing the pool below the dam, so decided to try another place. One hundred yards below the grist mill was the railroad

---

3 About 1902-1904.

4 Quoting John Ruskin, *Sesame and Lilies* (1865), "Of Queens' Gardens", § 85.

bridge, and below this a few rods a lumber mill called The Bootleg Mill. Why "Bootleg" I never learned. At any rate it bore no resemblance to any kind of footwear, and I have since thought that it may have been a rendezvous for bootleggers in prohibition[5] days—hence its name.

Beyond this was a shelving beach where I took my stand. I tied on a heavy lead sinker, then a big hook on which I threaded two or three fat angle worms, unrolled what I thought a suitable length of line, and cast out into the gentle current. I rested the tip of my pole on a rock that was conveniently handy, set the butt on the beach, and placed over it a good size boulder. Then I sat down and waited for a bite.

Perhaps fifteen long minutes rolled by. A freight train thundered over the bridge, leaving behind the silence of the rails, and the rippling of the river over its rock-strewn bed. Suddenly I saw my line straighten out, the tip of the pole bend to the surface of the water. I sprang to my feet, grasped the butt with one hand, with the other removed the rock, then, both hands clamped about the handle I gave a mighty pull and flung a gleaming fish far over my head up the beach. It was, I thought, a salmon; not as big as I had hoped for, but big for all that.

* * *

Where the fat, lubberly boy came from I know not. One moment invisible, the next he was on his knees over my precious fish. In a twinkling he tore the hook from its mouth, then rose to his feet, fish in hand, and started to run away. But he did not get far. I was after him like a thunderbolt, all my eighty-five pounds quivering with anger. I caught him about the neck, with my bent knee tripped him and flung him to the beach. My fish had fallen from his grasp, its mouth opening and closing spasmodically as though it were trying to ask what all the trouble was about.

The fat boy got slowly to his feet, his fists clenched. Then, to my amazement, he cried out: "My father will have you arrested! My father will put you in jail! My father works on the railroad!"

---

5 New Brunswick had prohibition in 1856, and from 1917-1927.

Evidently he desired to give me the impression that his father's vocation qualified him not only to have me arrested, but also to adjudicate the matter and jail me. At any rate his astonishing announcement failed to awe me properly. Instead, I pulled off my jacket and prepared to defend myself should he rush me.

But he didn't fight. He was too cowardly—although I was undersize for my age, and he topped my weight by twenty pounds. For a few moments he continued to glower at me, while he repeated over and over his former threat of arrest and imprisonment.

I made no reply, but stood on guard over my *salmon*. Finally, realizing that I was not to be intimidated, he thumbed his nose at me in the gesture that is as old as time, then turned and hastily made off.

I watched him until he was out of sight, then knocked my "salmon" over the head with a rounded beach rock, took it down to the river, washed the sand and gravel from its sides, wound up my line, and, pole in one hand and fish in the other, walked up the road flanking the Meduxnekeag to the footbridge, crossed to the north side, turned to the right and made my way to Queen Street where my father had his grocery shop. I had almost reached it when an old, bow-legged Negro—named Fred de Bois—halted me and said: "Say, boy, I'll give you fifteen cents for dat fish."

I was highly indignant. "No, siree," I replied, "not for fifteen dollars!" And although fifteen dollars was a fortune, I meant what I said. Had I not patiently angled for my prize and fought a boy who had threatened me with arrest for forcibly regaining my own property?

My father was busy with a customer. I proudly held up my fish to his gaze, but he merely nodded as though my catch were of no particular value. My pride a bit deflated, I left and proceeded homeward. Certainly my mother would show more enthusiasm! But when I entered the kitchen, held up my "salmon", and asked her to please cook it for dinner, she exclaimed in horrified tones: "A sucker! We never eat them over home—on the Miramichi! They're coarse fish! Please take it out in the garden, dig a *deep hole*, and bury it."

A sucker! A coarse fish! No one ate them on the Miramichi. If for no other reason, the fact that suckers were not considered suitable diet on the Miramichi was sufficient to condemn them anywhere else in the world.

And so a very disconsolate nine-year-old went to the tool-house where he got a spade, then to the garden, dug a *deep hole* and buried the fish he had fondly supposed was a salmon.

* * *

When I returned to the kitchen my mother's voice was very gentle as she said: "I'm sorry I spoke sharply to you. Now, wash your hands, dear, then have a molasses cookie." And she took from a bowl two of the golden disks she had just baked and set them on the table. They were a peace-offering, a salve to my bitter disappointment. As I ate I told her of the fat boy, and of his threat to have me arrested.

"Indeed!" she said. "What nonsense!" and there was a flash of resentment in her hazel eyes. Then she added, "I'm glad you stood up for your rights," and sealed her approval with a kiss on my cheek. Then she sat down in her rocking-chair and told me that the salmon is the bonniest fighter of all game fish; that it is born in the upper reaches of the river; stays there two, sometimes three years, then goes down to the sea where it grows big and fat. "And then," she went on, "when it is four or five pounds in weight, it returns to the same river—as a rule—where it spent its babyhood and childhood. Here it remains until autumn, when again it seeks the sea and, feeding on smelts, grows very fat. Then once more it speeds up its river— this time to reproduce its kind." She paused a few moments, then added in a dreamy voice: "I've been thinking it over, and when the holidays begin we'll go over home on a visit. You can fish for trout in the brook that runs through grandfather's farm, and not only see salmon, but have it almost every day for dinner."

"Oh," I cried excitedly, "trout!…and salmon! I can fish for trout, Mamma—every day?"

She smiled at my eagerness. "Of course, dear. I never say anything I don't mean. Any day—every day you wish."

She was that kind of a mother. So when the holidays began we went. I fished the brook to my heart's content and landed many trout. And some nights my grandfather and my uncles netted half a dozen silver salmon; and, for we lived off the land and what the river provided, we had salmon for dinner several times each week, and what was left over cold for supper. I remember it all as though it were yesterday—although then only ten years of age.[6]

---

6 He started this tale by saying he was nine years old.

— CHAPTER II —

THE MAIN SOUTHWEST MIRAMICHI[A]

During the evenings I heard much about the Main Southwest (as it was called) for my grandfather and my uncles had been to its very headwaters; but of the many important tributaries only the Bartholomew, the Renous, and the Dungarvon, stand out in my memory. Since then I have learned that south of the St. Lawrence the Main Southwest Miramichi is only exceeded in size and length by the Saint John River. Its extreme sources are the South and the North Branches; the latter heading from large springs only a couple of miles from the River de Chute, which vents into the Wapske—or to give it its full Indian name—*Waps-ke-hegan*. This in turn empties into the Main Tobique River.

The North Branch received numerous small branches such as Beaver, Frank's, The Sisters, Fifteen Mile, Bedell, and West Brooks. Salmon go as far as the Big Falls; and trout in abundance may be taken in all the brooks and dead waters. There is splendid trout fishing in Bedell Brook,[7] where some attain to great size, often going to three, and even five pounds.

* * *

---

7 Today called Beadle Brook.

A The old Micmac name for the Miramichi was *Lus-ta-goo-chick* (Little Restigouche)— *chick* being Micmac for little.

Six Salmon Rivers and Another

Fishing, hunting, the woods, were in my blood. But it was many years—following a varied career—before I fished the Miramichi.

How well I remember the day our professor of chemistry and physics at the Medico-Chirurgical College, Philadelphia—after his well meant but futile efforts to persuade me to remain in that city—finally said: "Well, Clarke, good luck." And he shook my hand in farewell.

Good luck. Since then I have heard the words on many salmon streams: "Good luck! A tight line!"

* * *

One late afternoon in August, 1916, having fished up Bedell Brook, and taken several nice pan trout averaging eight to twelve inches in length,*(5)* my guide turned the dugout canoe and we began our return to the camp situated on the upper angle of land where Bedell vents into the Miramichi. Bill was paddling along at a moderate rate, when seeing what I thought might be a likely spot for trout, I hurriedly cast my *Red Ibis* far to the right. No sooner had it touched the water than a huge sea trout curved out of the amber depths. It either missed my lure or refused it. The next moment we were past the spot; and although Bill backed up and I cast over it for several minutes, and even tried other flies, Leviathan refused to come again. Bill shook his head and said sadly: "That was a five-pounder. Too bad." Then he added, generously—in the effort to lessen my disappointment—"I was going too fast. My fault. Sorry."

I told him not to feel badly. I didn't. Perhaps I had taken the fly away from the fish... But that magnificent rise is forever photographed on my memory. I can see the water part, as though a boulder had reversed the law of gravity, and hurtled out of the brown water; see the small head and long, tapering body of the fish—even the carmine and gold spots along its side—the spread of its broad tail; then, as it completed its curve and sank back into the pool, see the slowly decreasing circles where it had made its plunge back into its native element.

*   *   *

From Bedell the North Branch pursues a leisurely course for some nine miles to the Forks—so called because here the South Branch conjoins to form the Main Southwest Miramichi.

At the Forks there is a very good salmon pool; but at present—due to easy access by motor cars—it (as well as the rest of the open water, as far down as Half Moon Cove) is over-fished. Forty years ago it was quite different. The fish were more plentiful, anglers few. At the beginning of August, 1916, I took my sister[8] with me and drove over the then almost impassable road from Glassville to the Forks. *(4a-b)* Here Murdoch MacKenzie lived and had a set of camps, guides and dugout canoes. *(4a, 7b)* For the most part his sports preferred the river up to Boiestown—a distance of fifty miles through rough water environed by the most magnificent and awe-inspiring wilderness scenery in New Brunswick.

My sister and I stayed at the Forks two weeks. I was then a mere novice in the art of casting, hooking, and playing a salmon; and I have yet much to learn. As Walton has so sagely said: "For angling may be said to be so like the mathematics, that it can never be fully learnt, at least not so fully, but that there will still be more new experiences left for the trial of other men that succeed us." And again: "As the art of fencing was not to be taught by words, but by practice; and so must angling."

Nevertheless, green as I was in those early days, I took twenty-five salmon and grilse, and lost I remember not how many. *(6a-b)* During this time I saw but three other anglers among whom I divided the greater number of my catch. One of them was a lumberjack, river driver, and guide, as season and occasion offered. His name was Angus MacCormack. He kept his few homemade flies in a tin box which (when he left the Forks) he always deposited in a hollow pine stump on the south shore immediately in front of a warden's camp, the sills and studding of which were of hand-hewn timbers.

---

8   With them were two friends, Henry Wilson and a woman possibly nicknamed "Pete".

Six Salmon Rivers and Another

* * *

In 1921, when three angling friends and I purchased this camp from its owner, we extended the eastern end to make bedrooms, and built a wide verandah on the river side.*(7b)* Since the camp was situated on sloping ground the floor of the verandah was some six feet above the narrow bank of the stream. It was upheld by cedar logs or puncheons set into the sandy soil, and enclosed Angus MacCormack's pine stump in which he kept his fly box. For some reason Angus had permanently left this part of the river.

Unfortunately for the stability of the camp, two years after we had acquired it, I discovered some flints and broken arrowheads which had been upturned from their original depth when the workmen dug holes for the verandah puncheons.

There was a spade in the camp which I now used to do some excavating. I soon came on a layer of flints which led upwards to Angus's pine stump; beneath the tap roots I found a stone spearhead, a knife, and some arrowheads. Finally I dug out the whole of the big stump (which was almost three feet in diameter) and excavated even beyond it to within a foot of some of the puncheons, both camp and verandah settled alarmingly towards the river, and it cost forty-five dollars to have it jacked back into place. My co-partners claimed—with justice—that it was my fault; but I told them that I had spent a week digging, had unearthed some very precious prehistoric artifacts, and that they were therefore obliged—in the interest of palaeology—to make their contribution towards re-establishing the camp on its original foundation. Then I added that I was only joking; I'd pay for having the work done. But they would not consider this. Actually the high freshet was responsible for the damage; the camp should not have been built on a side hill anyway... Of course I was quite mad in occupying my time with digging when a good pool was aching to be fished; yet, since I was furthering the knowledge of palaeology—whatever that was—they were quite determined to make a suitable contribution, and be damned.

Since then I have discovered an important prehistoric campsite a couple of hundred yards east of the camp, unearthed some sixty beautiful arrowheads, many scrapers, knives, adzes, and other artifacts... Yes; the aboriginal inhabitants of north central New Brunswick knew well that the Main Southwest Miramichi River was filled with salmon; and that the vast wilderness—with its lakes, dead waters, and barrens—the habitat of moose, caribou, bear, as well as the beaver and lesser valuable fur-bearing creatures.

* * *

In August, nineteen-twenty, Doctor Grant and I spent a wonderful week at the Forks, taking several good salmon and grilse. But we were plagued by a local angler who—although he had fished the Forks Pool all summer—persisted in arising before daybreak, and, slipping past our camp in his canoe, preempted this piece of water. There was nothing for us to do but forestall him. So once we got up at two-thirty a.m., packed a lunch, and went over to the bar that flanks the western side of the North Branch and the Forks Pool.

* * *

Doctor Nelson P. Grant—whose companionship I shared on several salmon streams for almost three decades—was one of the finest characters, as well as the most Christian gentleman I have ever known. *(9c, 15a-b)* For more than thirty-three years he tended the sick and gave comfort to the dying. His very entry into a sickroom brought cheer and confidence. He loved children and the aged, and they adored him. His smile was tender and comforting, and his brown eyes mirrored the gentle compassion of his understanding soul. Year after year he was the generous physician and staunch friend of scores of poor people from whom he would accept no fee for his services. Every Christmas he bought turkeys, and had his wife—who was imbued with the same charitable spirit—fill baskets with other good things and sent them to the needy. Nor did he let the world know of his benefactions. Of such, I say, is the Kingdom of Heaven.

Angling was his favourite and only recreation. He loved the informing quiet of a little river, and all the wild life his quick eyes discerned along its banks. Equally he loved the companionship of his angling friends, and said that this meant more to him then the lordliest salmon that ever rose to a fly.

On this night—of which I have already spoken—we built a little friendship fire on the beach, and sitting beside it talked of many things; poetry, and life, religion, and the mystery of death; and suddenly, gazing above the spirelike spruces towards the constellation of Canis Major, we saw within it the Dog Star or Sirius—the brightest star in the heavens—like a great beacon let down by a beneficent deity to herald the coming of the dawn.

We never forgot that night. It returned again and again in after-years during our conversation; and I believe that those revealing hours before the dawn drew us even closer together in friendship and understanding.

Neither of us held much to church dogma and all the minutiae of ritual; but in our talk that night mention was made of W. H. Blake's *A Fisherman's Creed* (1923), a copy of which I had given him a few months before. And we agreed that: "Of all man's duties to his neighbour the most sacred is to achieve the sum of his attainable happiness and go clad in it; how otherwise shall he pay his debt in spreading abroad this communicable thing?" And then, pointing to the myriad stars, and again quoting Blake, my friend said: "What a transcendent act of faith is needed to affirm that those are self-born and march unguided through the void."

* * *

There is good fishing in the Salmon Hole three-quarters of a mile below the Forks. The lower end is deep, and appropriately named the *Dungeon*. The fish here seldom take, but the upper end of the Hole usually produces one fish, or more. One day while a gentle rain was falling and I had gone up the North Branch, Doctor Grant and his guide, Murdoch MacKenzie, went down to the Salmon Hole. The Doctor had a new rod—a huge, greenheart affair,[9] which MacKenzie christened *Black Maria*. He was also using casts

---

9   Greenheart is a dense South American evergreen. It is extremely limber, but tends to break at the ferrule, so the best greenheart rods were made with spliced joints. Greenheart rods are heavier than cane, but considerably more powerful. http://www.bamboorodmaking.com/html/greenheart_rods.html

of the then new paragut[10]—made in Japan. The salmon were in a taking mood. The Doctor hooked half a dozen good fish, but whether he struck too hard with his heavy rod or whether the gut was imperfect, they all broke away. Then the disgusted MacKenzie said: "Let me try that rod, will you?" The rod was passed back to him and he began casting with the same tragic results: five more salmon were hooked and lost.

When two days later we left for home the doctor presented the Black Maria to MacKenzie, and for years after—until fire destroyed the store house—it rested against the wall condemned and unused. The following winter I sent to the Fraser Company at Montreal, and purchased two twelve-foot Hardy rods with steel centres: one for my friend, the other for myself. They gave us splendid service for several years on the Miramichi, Tobique, and Restigouche waters. Then we each got lighter rods.

One October day—after the angling season had ended—I was going down the Miramichi with young Levi Grant, to explore an old Indian campsite near Crooked Rapids. Coming to the lower part of the Salmon Hole, we let the canoe drift sideways over its placid bosom. Near the head of the Dungeon the bottom was floored with fully three hundred salmon—big and little. They moved lazily to right and left as we got nearer. I have seen many salmon in my life, both in and out of the water, and I'm sure that on this day I saw eight or ten that would go thirty pounds, although save on three occasions I have never known such large fish to be taken so far up this river. They are generally all from twelve to fifteen pounds, a few twenty, and are active fighters. The grilse are small, usually three pounds.

The Salmon Hole is my favourite fishing ground on these upper reaches; however, it is no good in high water being wholly a low water pool.

* * *

One evening the Doctor, Larry, and I, were seated on the wide verandah of our camp talking and watching—as so many times before—the North Branch swinging on its age-old course around the bend to mingle its waters

---

10 Paragutta, a rubber-like material derived from rubber and gutta percha.

with those of the South Branch. After a while I said: "Would you chaps like to hear about Mrs. Fairfax's experience at the Salmon Hole?"

Both were willing to hear the story; Larry suggested that, before I began, we'd better have a little *touch*.

We had the little *touch*: some *Johnny Walker* and spring water. Then I began; but, if the reader wants to read of it he must—as Fielding would have said—do so in the next chapter.

— CHAPTER III —

THE WAY TO UNDERSTANDING[11]

Russell Boyer moved quickly forward and seated himself on the wide thwart behind the woman in the bow of the canoe, released the rope holding the lead anchor to the stern and allowed it to slip through the pulley until the lead found bottom, then fastened the rope around the cleat on the inner side of the gunwhale.

Mrs. Fairfax had turned him a startled, questioning look as the canoe, robbed of its momentum downstream, rocked and swung a little to right and left like a restive colt, the current rippling and gurgling along its sides. His brief: "It's all right, Mrs. Fairfax; we fish here," had reassured her. And now that he was seated behind her, and the added weight forced the bow downwards, the canoe lay in a line with the current that flung itself noisily against submerged boulders and finally smoothed itself out again in a dark pool flanked on the right by a small gravelly beach.

For a few moments the woman let her eyes rove over the tree-lined shores: spruces, maples, yellow birch and poplars, with here and there a white birch—like a slim dryad come to view her loveliness in the pellucid depths of the pool. From some hidden bower a thrush loosed a few flawless

---

11 This story was originally published in *The Canadian Home Journal*, July 1931. The two versions are identical but for a few words.

notes, then ceased—as though he had expired from the sheer ecstasy of his emotions—and, save for the rush of the water, quiet reigned over the river and the forest—a quiet broken only by the thin hum of mosquitoes as they flew about the woman's head.

"Better put some dope on," advised the guide, and proceeded to light the pipe he had filled. The smoke, strong and pungent, stung her nostrils. "Is it really necessary?" she inquired.

"Unless you want to be ate up," he returned with dispassionate directness.

She frowned and reached for the dope bottle beside her. "I was thinking that your tobacco might do for them," she said.

"Not unless you smoke too, Mrs. Fairfax."

She repressed the curt retort that rose to her lips, and taking off her long gloves drew the cork, poured some of the evil-smelling mixture into one palm, and anointed her face.

"Better put some on the back of your neck," he advised; "one got you there—already."

She sighed resignedly. "I suppose it is necessary," she said coldly, and turned him her eyes. "Is no one immune? I mean—" as he looked blank—"do they bite anyone?"

He blew out a cloud of smoke that caused her to cough and quickly turn her head. He said, "Only one I ever knew was a parson. He was—what you call it?—immune. P'raps he smelled of the brimstone he so often preached about. At any rate they bit him but didn't poison...*Holy Piscator*," he cried, "did you see *that*?" Not waiting for an answer, he went on excitedly, "A salmon, Mrs. Fairfax; big as a yearlin' heifer. He jumped down there opposite the leanin' spruce."

"Oh," she said languidly, "I didn't see it. Are you sure?" she added carelessly.

"Certain. Must have been the big fellow Mr. Fairfax raised last evening. He said it was a big one. Unless—" he pursued, "this is another. Accordin' to Bill Sommers quite a run is on the way up. They passed Hayes' Bar a week ago. Should be here now, Mrs. Fairfax—"

She picked up her rod. "What fly had we better put on?" she said abruptly.

"Jock Scott," he answered. "Nothing like a Jock: unless"—he puffed rapidly at his pipe—"it'd be a Nighthawk, or a Silver Doctor. Let's see it—" he reached for her rod, and picked out a fly from the box beside him—"I'll tie on a jock; double six." He tested the leader, and began tying on the fly, puffing at his pipe and muttering to himself.

* * *

I paused in my narrative and the Doctor said: "It's getting interesting. Go on, please. I'm anxious for the thrills. You're telling it well." And Larry joined in, "Was Mrs. Fairfax a good looker? I rather think so—Go on, let's have the works."

"Beautiful," I answered. "And actually a good head. Been spoiled a bit, I'd say…"

Well, she waited while Russell tied on her fly, her blue eyes fixed far down on the converging shores into which the river winked its course and was lost to further view. Ronald Fairfax—her husband of less than a year! And they had quarrelled—a few hours after arriving at the cabin. Their first evening on the river! *His* river, he called it, from long association with its miles of rapids and still reaches. He had gone upriver with his guide this morning without kissing her; his only words as he stepped into his canoe: "I hope you won't be too bored, Janet." And to Russell Boyer, her brown-faced guide: "You should rise something in the Salmon Pool, Russ."

Seated comfortably in the bow of the canoe, she had watched with smarting eyes the shores rapidly slip past to the accompaniment of her guide's paddle, and her own disturbing thoughts. Of course she had been to blame, but Ronald shouldn't have insisted on her accompanying him on this trip. Perhaps, though, had she been less tired from the long train journey and the subsequent twenty-eight miles through monotonous farm and forest land in a wheezy car, she would have been more sporty about it all. But the knowledge that she had been a poor sport did not hurt half as much as the consciousness that Ronald was disappointed in her.

* * *

They had arrived at MacKenzie's lodge—a dull place of logs with a mosquito-netted verandah—a couple of hours before dark, and Ronald's guide had immediately suggested going down to the Salmon Hole. She remembered her husband's "All right, Bill," and the light in his eyes as, turning to her, he had said, "Would you like to come, Janet?"

Why had she refused? She didn't know, unless it was by way of protest against the expedition from the very beginning. His face had gone blank. "Oh, well—" he had begun. She had said, hastily, "Please go; don't mind me. I—I'm quite tired." He had gone gladly; it seemed, as though angling were the most important thing in the world.

Sitting there on the verandah, with the mosquitoes flinging themselves madly against the screen, she had watched twilight slowly settling over the river, over the forest beyond, so that the pyramidal spruces and pines stood out in the half light like enormous Chinese pagodas. Somewhere in the woods beyond the little clearing in which the lodge stood, an owl had sent out its questioning "*Ka-hoo-agh!*" like some mysterious spirit voicing its derision at man's inanities. Her guide had come down from the guides' cabin, made a fire in the stove, then noisily begun to set the table in the little dining-room. A dark-skinned taciturn, uninteresting fellow, she thought; always smoking a pipe, from which he inhaled and blew out volumes of vile smoke.

Occasionally she had peered obliquely through the screen downriver, hoping to see her husband returning. All she saw was the hurrying current, its surface broken by numerous small fish: parr, the guide Russell had said (whatever they were), rising after a late hatch of flies. Opposite the lodge was the Forks Pool, she had heard. She didn't care. It was all unspeakably dreary; so primitively wild that her heart ached for contact with the civilization she had always known and loved. Back there the city would be aglow with countless lights, people hurrying to theatres, clubs. In fancy she could see it all—

Why did men come to such places as this? Miles and miles from anywhere! Fish?—one could purchase them at the market. Ronald had assured her she would enjoy it— What? It was possibly all right for Indians and such half-civilized white creatures as their guides. But her husband—?

What was it in men that made them long to go off to such remote places? Some inherited primitive instinct, she supposed.

It had been long after dark when Ronald returned, quite boyishly excited at having risen an enormous fish. He (why did men always speak of fish as though they were all of the male sex?) had come twice for the fly. "Perhaps," Ronald had continued, "I took it away from him, the last time. Bill thinks so." He had turned to Bill.

The guide had paused in the lighting of his pipe, the glow from the match causing the oil on his face to glisten. "Yes," he had said, "he meant bizness. Should-a let him have it." Then dispassionately, "Oh well, he'll take tomorrer." He had turned to her, "P'raps you'll hook him when you go down in the mornin'."

* * *

After supper they had all sat on the verandah and talked. Sitting there beside her husband in the dark, she had heard more about the life history of salmon than she had ever thought could be known, let alone remembered. Perhaps half of what they said was pure fabrication. Preposterous to talk about mere salmon as though they were possessed of intelligence, and surrounding them with an aura of romance that, if anything, was childish.

Later, after the guides had left, Ronald had said, "I say, Janet, you're frightfully quiet. Sleepy?"

How surprised he had been when she told him that she wasn't happy in this wilderness. "It—the quiet—everything—has got on my nerves," she added in a low voice.

"Oh dear!" he had cried: "I'm awfully sorry. I had hoped—thought you'd like it up here. I've been hugging myself, and saying, 'How Janet will enjoy this!' You see, my dear, I've so much wanted us to have kindred likes." And then, after a few moments of strained silence, "Lots of women go angling with their husbands. I—I'm sorry."

She had countered with, "You're inconsistent, Ronald. You say you want us to have kindred likes—but *I* like tennis, and you don't. You have no more right to ask me to like *your* woods and river than I have to insist that you like tennis."

"All right," he had said, "I'll take you home tomorrow."

But at this she had protested. "No, I'll stay and see it through." She had flushed there in the dark at his icy remark, "And make a martyr of yourself."

Odd, and woefully tragic, that on this, their first vacation together since their honeymoon, almost a year ago, they had quarrelled, and about fishing, of all things. She was sorry she had allowed herself to voice her dislike of the river, told herself she should have quietly endured all the discomforts without murmur. She had been on the point of apologizing and asking him to think no more about it, when he had said, "I had thought we'd have been good pals." Indeed there *had been* genuine pathos in his voice, like that of a little boy who has been denied some coveted toy. Yet she was deeply hurt. "You're disappointed in me," she had said.

* * *

She remembered, now, while waiting for Russell to hand her the rod, and the mosquitoes hummed about her face and sought out portions unanointed with fly-dope, how she had lain there on her little screened cot far into the night, thinking her thoughts to the interminable fluting and croaking of the frogs over in the Bogan;[12] telling herself again and again that men were selfish and unreasonable, and that she had been a fool for consenting to come on this trip. Tragic—yes; all the more so since she loved Ronald... Disappointed in her! Well, at least she had been honest about it all...

I paused in my story, and Larry said: "In my opinion her husband's remark was rather brutal. Of *course* it implied he was disappointed in her. Naturally, she was hurt."

"You know," the Doctor joined in, "it's almost always difficult for most people to appreciate the other fellow's preference for his own particular form of sport. Personally—until I'd argued the matter out with myself—I thought it childish for people to knock a golf ball about for hours at a time. Of course this Janet Fairfax—as she admitted to herself—should have

---

12 In New Brunswick a bogan is a narrow stream winding through marshy land to a lake or river.

played the game while it lasted. And Ronald, instead of blowing up like a petulant ten-year-old, should have taken her in his arms and gently told her that he understood her point of view, and that in future he'd not insist on her taking part in his form of sport. That would have set matters right. The trouble with us poor humans—who imagine we are so wise—is that we haven't yet learned how to play the game; and the result is often disastrous."

"Right," agreed Larry. Then to me, "Before you go on about Mrs. Fairfax—whom I like—how about another little "touch" all around?"

I said no. I wanted a clear head for my story. The Doctor, however, had a little touch. Then I went on:

Russell's voice: "Here you are, Mrs. Fairfax," and his hand holding out her rod, awakened her from her painful reverie. She took it. "I'll likely hook you," she said.

"Wouldn't be the first time I'd been hooked," he remarked cheerfully. Then added, "There was a fellow I guided last year, hooked me in the ear; both barbs clean through."

"What did you do?" she asked, a little interested.

"Swore bohemiously," he replied. "Lucky I had a pair of cutting pliers in my kit. He had to snip off the barbs, and push the hooks back, then I was free. I—" He paused. Her peals of laughter echoed against the wooded shore. "Wasn't any laughing matter at the time," he said, but chuckled good naturedly.

She sobered. "I beg your pardon," she said. "I was amused at your swearing bohemiously. I'd never heard the expression." And she decided to be nice to him.

"I'm pretty good at it," he admitted.

"What shall I do with it, now it's all rigged up?" she asked, holding up the rod.

The tone of his voice, more than the words, conveyed his dismay. "Mean to say you've never cast a fly, Mrs. Fairfax?"

"No," she admitted. "And I haven't been anxious to try."

"Good Gawd!" he ejaculated. "I didn't know that! Mr. Fairfax said you'd never hooked a salmon; but of course I thought you'd at least fished for trout!... Well, let me tell you, Mrs. Fairfax, your education's been neglected. 'Course some of 'em's like that when they first come; but I thought—being Mr. Fairfax's wife, you'd know *something* about the game."

She flushed painfully, bit her lip. The cheek of him to talk to her like that—as though she were a child! Certainly these guides were ignorant and should be made to keep their place— Too familiar. She'd ask to have another guide on the morrow.

"Salmon fishing—" was saying oracularly—"is the sport of kings. I've guided lords, and dukes, bishops, archbishops, and lesser church dignitaries. Millionaires. And they all liked it. Liked it, did I say? Why, Mrs. Fairfax, one of 'em said he didn't want to go to heaven if there was no fishing there."

She smiled, and said, "Of course it wasn't one of the church dignitaries who said that."

Russell nodded. "A bishop, no less," he averred soberly. Then he added, "At any rate, Mrs. Fairfax, you can't find any better fish stories than in the Bible. You remember how the Master told his disciples, who were catching no fish, to put their net on the other side of the boat, and they got as many as it would hold! I believe that, but, that story of Jonah being swallowed by the whale, I can't take. For why—? Well, the acid in a whale's stomach—just like in a salmon's—is so strong that poor Jonah couldn't have existed in it more'n a few hours, certainly not three days! He'd have been no better than hog mash."

She was laughing again, peals of musical laughter like silver bells ringing. He said, "You hand me the rod, Mrs. Fairfax, and I'll show you how to cast."

Obediently, and now much taken with his talk, she passed the butt of the rod backward. Again the thrush sang, and from farther down the stream a white-throat lifted his voice in his assurance that: "It's good — good! — good! — to-be-here! dear!"

* * *

"For myself," said Russell, as he stood up behind her and made a short cast to the right, "each year when April comes, and all the little brooks are awake, and rushing like happy children to join the big river, I think of this bit of water, and my hands itch to hold a paddle, or cast a fly— You cast first to the right, Mrs. Fairfax, let the fly sink a little, and swing round with the current 'till it's on a line with the bow. Then you make another cast to the left, and do the same. That's the way you cover all your water— One time I thought I'd go to the city and get work. New York, it was. Got a job handling freight in a wholesale establishment— Now you pull another two feet of line off the reel, and make another cast to the right— S'long's it was winter I didn't mind the city too much; but directly April come I got hankering for home. I could smell the trees, hear the brooks chattering, the birds singing, the piping of the frogs. Then one day I heard a flock of wild geese honking their way northward far over the roofs of the city. That settled it— Now to the left—I went to the boss, and said, 'Sun's high in the sky,' I said. 'I'm leaving for home last of the week.'

"'What the blazes do you mean, Russell? Sun's high in the sky! Of course it is. What's that got to do with going home?—' Two more feet, Mrs. Fairfax, and to the right. I don't expect to get a rise till we make the next drop, but we always start in here—— I says to the boss, 'That's just it. Sun's high in the sky; days getting warmer; river's free of ice, fish running up to the spawning grounds. I gotta go.' 'You're a good man,' he says; 'if it's more wages you want, I'll—' But I says 'No it isn't that. Something more than that; it's a hankering!' And I told him about the river. 'You're a fool, Russell,' he said— Now to the left again... No, that was a trout, Mrs. Fairfax— 'You stay here,' he said, 'and you'll be foreman before long.' 'No,' I replied, 'I wouldn't stay if you made me president of the concern. I'm going back the last of the week.' 'Well, then,' he said, laughing, 'you come back when the sun gets *low* in the sky, and I'll give you back your job. Perhaps raise you.' But I didn't go. No, and I don't intend to... You taking notice how I cast, Mrs. Fairfax—? All right. I'll fish this drop, then, when we move down, you can try it."

* * *

She had been more interested in his recital of his New York trip than in his casting and the accompanying words of instruction. He was certainly an oddity, giving up a good job with chances of advancement, to return to this wilderness. Yet she was beginning to like him a lot. There had been deep feeling in his voice as he talked that proclaimed him not merely a lover of fishing, but of the woods as well. Strange, that the lure of angling so got into men's blood that they were willing to endure all manner of discomforts to indulge it! Ronald—she flushed—was like that. As childlike as this strange man behind her, casting so patiently with such meticulous care, now to the right, now to the left, as though his life depended on it. Such an uninteresting and profitless pastime. She didn't believe there was a fish in the river bigger than a trout. Then she remembered that Ronald had raised a salmon last night. Last night—Ah! She wished she could erase all that had been said from her mind—from both their minds. She said:

"I can't understand what pleasure you get out of casting—casting. You don't even catch a little fish."

"You wouldn't understand," Russell returned, "not being an angler. As for the little ones—if I wanted trout I'd put on a parmachene-belle. Anyway, if you could hook a salmon every cast, the game would soon lose its interest. It's the anticipation that makes it worth while, the feeling that at any moment a fish will strike, and the reel go singing like mad. It's like any other game, Mrs. Fairfax."

"I see," she said doubtfully. "Well, I'd like to see *something* break the monotony."

"There you go," he said, "talking like some others I've guided. But when it comes—a strike, I mean—you forget all about the hours of casting and waiting."

* * *

She noted that he now had out an astonishing lot of line; seventy-five feet, or more. When he retrieved it to make another cast it described a beautiful arc far back of him. She noted that he waited until it had straightened out, then threw it diagonally across the stream, the fly alighting on the water with scarcely a ripple. She wondered if Ronald could cast like that. Very likely, since he had been fishing for years.

"My husband," she said, "does he cast as well as you?"

The Way To Understanding

"Um—yes," answered Russell, "Mr. Fairfax is one of the best anglers I've known."

"Thank you," she murmured. And she didn't ask herself why his answer gave her so much pleasure. He was reeling in now.

A thrill passed over her. "Oh!" she cried, "have you got one?"

He laughed. "No—if I had you'd know it without asking," he remarked with emphasis. "We'll make a drop, now, then you can take the rod." He laid it in the bottom of the canoe, and lifted the anchor rope.

She felt the canoe slipping downward, come to a quivering standstill. "Now," he said, handing her the rod, "you try. Don't try too hard. Just swing your rod backward—about twenty degrees, and then throw the line to the right… That's it; not bad. Let the fly sink a little and swing with the current— There, now to the left. Pretty good— You did that quite well. Pull about two feet of line from the reel and start all over."

"I'm afraid I'll hook you—" she began.

"Never mind me," he advised serenely; "I'll risk the hooking."

She gave a low laugh. It would be almost worth it to hear him swear bohemiously. What an odd and apt expression; she thought. A little trout made a dart at the fly, leaping out of the water and falling back with a splash. She gave an excited squeal: "Oh, I almost had it!" Russell only said, "Cast to the left. You don't want to hook that." She obeyed. Then she stripped more line from the reel and again cast. The trout had sent her pulse hammering, and she hoped it would decide to take the fly. Of course she was making a muddle of this casting business. Try as she would she couldn't make it alight on the water as the guide did. Could she ever acquire his seemingly effortless sureness?

"By the Super-Sally-Co-Ajical!" he cried. "Did you see *that*?"

She wondered if his strange expletive was a sample of his bohemious profanity. "Reel in quick!" he commanded.

She did so, wonderingly. She had noticed nothing unusual. "That's enough," he said; "hand me the rod. We'll rest him, Mrs. Fairfax."

She half turned and glanced at him. His eyes shone, and as he removed the plug of tobacco from his breast pocket, the hand holding it shook a little. "What was it?" she asked.

"You raised a fish, Mrs. Fairfax; a beauty. You didn't see him?" She shook her head.

"I saw him make a boil beneath the surface. I think," he added, "he saw the fly just as you were drawing it up to make another cast. We'll give him a fiver, Mrs. Fairfax." And, knife opened, Russell began to cut some of the tobacco into the hollow of his left hand.

"A fiver—?" she questioned.

"A rest," he explained. "We always rest a salmon after he misses the fly. They're different from trout. Aristocrats, like dukes, and lords, and gentlemen that aren't neither. You see, salmon don't take the fly because they're hungry. They don't eat until they go back to the sea. I've opened hundreds, and I've never seen anything in their stomachs but a little brown liquid." He paused, and having rubbed the tobacco to the desired fineness, slowly began to fill his pipe.

"That's odd," she said. "Why do they take a fly then?" He had struck a match, and as he cupped his hands to shield the flame from the draft, and held it over the bowl of his pipe, emitted a cloud of smoke. With a flip of his hand he tossed the match into the stream and said, "Some say it's because the fly bothers 'em, and they want to kill it. And yet," he continued reflectively, "there's experts who say it does eat. But you can take it from me, Mrs. Fairfax, the salmon's the cleanest living of any fish. A real aristocrat. Fights like one, too. That's what makes him such sport. Never know just what he'll do, either before or after he's hooked… Better put on some more fly-dope, Mrs. Fairfax; the flies are bad."

* * *

She did as he advised, anointing her face and the back of her neck. It was unpleasant smelling stuff but since it kept the flies from biting her, it must be endured. She let her eyes rest on the pool below her; a few small trout were breaking its surface. Doubtless there were salmon in its depths since Russell had asserted that one had risen to her fly. Being an experienced guide, it was hardly possible he had made a mistake. He had been quite excited and, she must admit, had imparted to her a wistful desire to hook the fish and experience the thrill he had assured her would be in store for her. There *must* be something in the game, or men wouldn't travel hundreds of miles to engage in it. She thought of Ronald—of his words: "I'd hoped we would be good pals." She wanted to be a pal to him—more than anything else in the world. Of course he had been unreasonable in expecting her to enjoy all the things he did. Love of any game was purely a personal matter; and angling was essentially a man's game. Still, she felt she would give worlds to have had stilled her feelings last night. Having come, she should have endured the wilderness for the few days they had planned to be there, and then, any future time made excuses and remained home…

"All right. Let him have it," said her guide's voice in her ear. He handed her the rod. "Throw the fly as easy as you can," he advised.

She released the fly from the little ring above the reel and made a cast to the right, observed the line swing with the current. She heard the voice behind her say, "Never mind casting to your left. Strip off a little more line, Mrs. Fairfax. He raised farther down." She did so, and again cast, eagerly watched the fly describe its half circle, the while her heart hammered in an unwonted manner. Would the salmon rise again, or was he one of those easily satisfied creatures? Perhaps the fault lay in her casting. Possibly if Russell were to take the rod— But, if the game were worth playing she'd like to play it herself—experience all the thrills— The fly was now on a line with the bow of the canoe. "Shall I strip off more line?" she asked.

"Yes."

The reel sang a few staccato notes as she drew out a few more feet. Then, as deftly as she could, she made another cast.

"I think that'll reach," said her guide with barely repressed excitement.

Again she watched the fly swing downstream. Then, as the line straightened out, she was conscious of a mighty upheaval of water. Her heart seemed to pop into her throat, an electric tingle ran up her arms. For an instant she saw a broad tail emerge, the head and curved body of an enormous fish, then, even as she automatically lifted the rod tip, the reel's discordant notes rang in her ear.

The pliant rod bent double. As in a dream she heard and obeyed Russell's roared command to keep her hand off the reel. "Let him run!" he cried exultantly. "Keep the tip up—higher yet! That's it—" The reel was shrieking out its glad music. She could see the line far down the pool, cutting the water like the thin blade of a knife, but of the salmon no sign. Her heart was beating tumultuously beneath the butt of the rod pressed against her side. Her ears rang as though she had drunk some potent elixir. Then, even as she obeyed Russell's command to drop the tip of her rod, she saw the salmon leap far out of the water, hang poised for a breathless second on the curved summit of its leap, and then fall back with a splash that sent up showers of foam.

"Reel in! Reel!—he's coming upstream. Don't let him get slack line!"

She obeyed, reeling frantically, thinking: "Oh, this is glorious! I mustn't lose him— now!"

"Easy—easy—take your hand off—he wants to go again. Keep the tip up! Ah, he's going to leap again in a moment. Don't lose your head. There—drop the tip—"

Again she saw the fish leap straight into the air, an arc of polished silver, to strike the water on its side with a sound like breaking glass. Before she had a chance to again drop her tip it had repeated its performance, to the guide's chortle of delight: "Go it, Silversides! That'll take the steam out of you."

Silversides, she thought, that was a splendid name for the beautiful dynamic creature on the other end of her line. She understood now why men came hundreds of miles, and endured all manner of discomforts. Tennis—? Any other game she knew was tame compared to this. No wonder Ronald had been disappointed—

But where was the fish going? Far off down the mirrorlike pool, she could see the line cutting the water. Was the salmon bent on going back to the sea? She glanced down at her reel and saw with dismay that little line remained. But, even as she breathed out an agonized, "Oh—oh, I'll lose him!" she was conscious that Russell had pulled up his anchor and was paddling after the speeding fish. "Reel in. Retrieve as much line as you can!" he cried. "Keep the rod high! All right; stop reeling—he's turned—going across the pool."

* * *

She was glad for the respite; her muscles ached; perspiration—mingled with fly-dope—streamed into her eyes, smarting and almost blinding her. She dashed a gloved hand over her face, saw the salmon leap close to the left shore, and mechanically dropped the tip of her rod. She heard Russell say, "That's right, Mrs. Fairfax. No one could do it better." A wave of pride swept over her. What a splendid fellow he was! And she had thought him crude, uninteresting, entirely lacking in courtesy. "Thank you, Russell," she murmured. "Do you think we'll really land him?"

"No knowing, Mrs. Fairfax; I've had 'em all played out, ready for the gaff,[13] and then seen them get away. But it's all in the game. If we lose, we lose."

"Of course," she panted through set lips. But she didn't want to lose— Not this time— Her first salmon. It would be tragic. It had swung to the centre of the pool now, where it sank to the bottom. She could hear her taut line hum like a bowstring after the shaft is sped. She wondered what it was doing down there. She asked Russell.

"Boring," he answered. "Got his nose down in the gravel trying to get rid of the hook. Or p'raps resting beside some rock, jerking his head from side to side. Jigging, we call it. Either way it's dangerous; apt to work the hook loose, or break the cast. I'll telegraph him."

She wondered what he meant. The strain on her arms was becoming almost unbearable; she felt they must soon drop from exhaustion. From the corner of her eye she saw Russell's hand, holding his heavy jack-knife, reach over her shoulder and strike the handle of the rod, above the reel, a few sharp blows. "Watch out, now, Mrs. Fairfax, he'll go like hell!"

---

13   A pole with a sharp hook on the end, used to stab a large fish and lift it into the boat or onto shore. http://en.wikipedia.org/wiki/Fishing_gaff

The salmon did. It rushed downstream with the speed of a thunderbolt, rose in a skittering leap that spurned up the water like a racing motor-boat, turned a somersault, then sank to the bottom and renewed its jigging tactics. "Oh," she breathed, "he's at it again! What shall we do, Russell?"

"Fight," he muttered; "nothing else to do. Want me to take the rod?"

"No—No, thank you," she panted. "I—I'd rather do it—myself." But could she? Her left hand, clamped about the handle of the rod, seemed powerless to relax even had she wished, while her right fluttered about the reel in an agony of indecision whether or not to wind up. Every muscle and sinew ached; and instead of showing signs of exhaustion, the salmon seemed as fresh and strong as when first hooked. Indeed, she wondered if she might be the first to give in.

* * *

"I'm going to get below him and land you on that strip of beach," said Russell. "Reel in as fast as you can as we move down, and don't give him any slack... That's right. Keep the tip well up, and if he starts running, let go of the reel... Courage, Mrs. Fairfax."

The canoe was nearing the little beach, when suddenly, as though the salmon knew that now was the time to begin more dangerous tactics, it started straight for the canoe. Russell's command in her ear to reel faster was accompanied by a splash as he thrust down his long setting-pole, snubbing the canoe's downward course. "Tip higher! Higher," he cried. "And reel—"

She obeyed as best she could, though the muscles of her hand as she worked the reel handle ached excruciatingly. She could see the salmon now, not more than twenty feet distant. Suddenly it came to the surface and, bending its body in an arc, gave a slap at the leader with its tail. Hardly knowing why she did so, she took her fingers off the reel, and heard Russell's low, "That's right, Mrs. Fairfax. Now throw the rod tip hard to the left. That'll force his head down." It did, and the fish started up past them with a rush that made the rod tremble and bow in a half circle. "That's where we want him. Down quicker now. Let him run, Mrs. Fairfax. We'll land, and you can play him from the beach."

As the canoe touched the gravelly beach Russell leaped out, was by her side in an instant, and bending, grasped the gunwale with one hand and reached the other to steady her as she rose. "Now," he said, "step out. Careful; don't fall; and keep the rod high."

The solid earth seemed unreal to her feet. She staggered a little, but kept her balance and her eyes on the pool where the salmon was still boring upstream. Russell, having drawn up the canoe, came and stood beside her. She followed his advice as best she could. She pressed a gloved finger on the line and held the rod a little higher;*(8)* as the fish felt the added strain it half turned and she saw it upend, then it again disappeared. "Oh," she breathed, "is he gone?" Russell's voice reassured her. "Not too hard," he said, "just a little pressure on the line." She obeyed. Again the salmon made a big boil beneath the surface, then took a diagonal course across the pool to the opposite shore. The reel seemed to echo her own unspoken protest. Russell's voice, "Shallow water over there; try and turn him," sounded far off. And though she tilted the rod upstream, she felt that any effort of hers would be futile to stay that determined rush. Her arms ached with an almost intolerable fatigue; the pool danced bewilderingly before her eyes and, as she put more pressure on the line, her gloved finger burned as though it had come in contact with a red-hot brand… As in a dream she heard Russell tell her to reel in now, and was vaguely aware that she must have turned the salmon and that it was coming towards her. "Hurry! Back up!" cried Russell. And slipping, regaining her footing by a miracle, she retreated towards the line of trees, all the while reeling—reeling, now a full turn, then a half, until finally she brought up against the bushes.

Through a half-blinding mist she dimly saw Russell spring to the canoe and seize his long-handled gaff, then wade out into the stream until it was almost to his knees; a few yards beyond him glimpses of something, then the broad tail feebly churning the water. Then it again disappeared and took out a little more line. And although she sensed that the salmon was almost exhausted she realized, too, that the moment was fraught with danger, that victory still hung in the balance. Had not Russell told her he had seen fish about ready for the gaff, and then get away?

She could now see Russell more distinctly, his hands holding the extended gaff, like a statue symbolizing the very spirit of vigilance and expectancy. And, coming yet nearer, that which she knew was her salmon. Suddenly, she saw Russell strike, the water beat into foam as he drew the salmon towards him. Then, with the fish held high, he was stumbling towards the shore, face and eyes shining with triumph.

Still holding her rod she tottered slowly to meet him. Her knees trembled as though she had run a long race. Her lips framed foolish unspoken phrases; her heart was beating with a wild exultation. She felt the glad tears rush to her eyes; not so much because of her actual physical victory over the fish, as because of its significance in her future relations with her husband.

She heard Russell say in a matter-of-fact voice, "A nice fish. He'll go over twenty pounds; twenty-one, or two, I'd say." He picked up a stick from the beach and tapped the still struggling fish over the head, putting it out of its misery. Then he dipped it into the river, washed off the blood, laid it carefully on the beach in front of her, straightened and looked into her eyes. "You played a good game, Mrs. Fairfax," he said warmly.

She held out a trembling hand to him. "Thank you, Russell," she said. "I'd never have landed him if it hadn't been for your advice." And suddenly she felt for him that comradeship which comes to all men who have shared experience such as hers. Never would she forget this hour.

"My—my hand's dirty—" he protested, and wiped it off on the sleeve of his mackinaw.

She wondered that he made no comment about her previous indifference to angling.

She said, "Now I know why men make a religion of their fishing."

He smiled. "Want to try for another?" he asked.

"No, thank you, Russell," she answered; "not now—not until after lunch. I want to go back to my husband."

He nodded. "All right, Mrs. Fairfax." Taking her rod he wound up the line, and attached the hook to the little ring above the reel. Then he struck a match and lighted his pipe, picked up the salmon, deposited it in the bow of the canoe, pushed it off a little, steadied it until she was seated, then, setting pole in hand, he took his place behind her.

*   *   *

I ceased, my story ended.

I heard the Doctor draw a deep breath. "You know," he said, "you had me on tenterhooks. Of course I knew she wouldn't lose that fish— But, well—I often felt myself trembling. How about you, Larry?"

"The same—only more; I wanted to yelp. I say, Doc, (to me) is that a true story? Was there actually a Mrs. Janet Fairfax?"

"As true as I could make it," I replied. She *actually* existed—*only*—her name wasn't Fairfax."

"It doesn't matter," said Larry. "Now, how about a *touch*. A good one; and we'll drink to Janet Fairfax—or whatever her name is. And, of course—to Russell."

PHOTOGRAPHS

— PART ONE —

a. GFC's grandfather Moses Harris, c. 1907

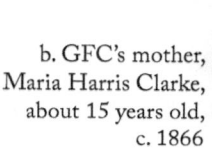

b. GFC's mother, Maria Harris Clarke, about 15 years old, c. 1866

c. GFC's daughter Dees fishing at Taffa Lake, about 5 years old, c. 1924

d. GFC's daughter Jane, about 4 years old, after catching a trout at the Forks, 1919 or 1920

a. GFC and friends camping, with rods, guns, axe, lantern and Victrola, c. 1902 GFC on left

b. GFC and friends camping at Jackson's Falls, on the Meduxnekeag River, 1904. GFC is second from left.

c. GFC and friends with trout, Jackson's Falls, 1904. GFC is on right.

a. GFC with trout, c. 1909

b. The St John River above Woodstock, summer 1964

c. Catching trout in winter, c. 1909

d. Fishing the Hartland pool, 1950s

e. The St John River north of Hartland, 1967

Murdoch Mackenzie and, in the car, L to R: Henry Wilson, GFC, Ruby Clarke and Ruby's friend "Pete"

b. Henry Wilson and GFC with a string of trout

Two weeks at the Forks of the Main Southwest Miramichi, June 1916

GFC with trout at the Forks of the Main Southwest Miramichi, June 27, 1916

a. Waiting for a rise

b. Netting a salmon

GFC at the Forks, c. 1916

a. The Forks of the Miramichi, looking upriver, 1971

b. Jane, Murdoch Mackenzie and Dees at the Forks c. 1925. The camp verandah is behind Dees.

c. The Forks in 1997, almost the same view as in the 1925 photograph

"Not too hard," he said, "just a little pressure on the line."

a. GFC holding 2 salmon, early 1920s

b. Anglers and guides, GFC and Noel Moulton in lead canoe

c. Dr Grant holding 2 salmon, 1920s

d. GFC, Bill Kennedy, Charlie Clark, probably October 1948

— CHAPTER IV —

THE MIRAMICHI CONTINUED

How many times my chums and I drove into the camp-yard at the Forks; and barely had we alighted when Harley Hannah opened the screen door of his camp, came out, greeted us with a warm shake of the hand, then helped us lug our dunnage down the little incline to our camp. Then he would hurry back to his own camp and return with an armful of split cedar kindlings, and a roll of birch bark he had stripped at some previous time from one of the many trees that line the tote-road near the Salmon Hole. "To start the fire with," he would say in his low, resonant voice… He used to spend a couple of months each year at the Forks. He loved it. He was one of the most kindly and charitable men it has been my privilege to know. Were a neighbour seriously ill Harley would go and sit up with him. Before he had a telephone he would harness his horse—be the season summer or winter—and go to town for the doctor or to get medicine. Several times, when I was ready to leave camp, he would ask me if I minded delivering two or three grilse he had caught that morning to some old people near his home. "You know," he would say, "they never get a salmon. They'll be pleased a lot."

* * *

One day a fish broke water in the Forks Pool. Harley was on our verandah at the moment and said: "Get your rod, Doctor, and I'll put you over on the bar."

We reached the beach; he pulled up his canoe and stood some distance back of me. As I fished and gradually lengthened out line, I turned and waved him farther back. He obeyed. A few moments later—as I wanted to cast yet farther—I again motioned him to move. He laughed and said: "You can't hook me where I am now," and took a few steps up the beach. I was not so sure. Suddenly, as I retrieved my line, waited for the back cast to straighten out and then swung my rod forward to make another cast, I felt a sharp tug back of me and heard Harley's voice: "You've got me, Doctor!"

I laid my rod on the beach and went to where he stood. Both hooks were firmly fixed in the muscle of his shoulder. Old Joe Nixon—the Warden—was standing on the south shore watching us, so I asked him to go into my camp, get a pair of wire-cutters; a bottle of whiskey, and a glass from the table and come over.

In a few minutes he handed it to Harley, and suggested he add some river water. He preferred, however, to drink it neat.

I had to force the barbs of the hook through the flesh, cut them off, then back the hook out.

Ten minutes later, while I was still casting, I heard him give a whoop, then say: "You couldn't do that again, Doctor—could you?" The anaesthetic had worked and he was ready for another hook in the shoulder—or anywhere else…

A few years later an angler came up from the Salmon Hole with a double hook through his upper lip, and three years ago one of my guests—a famous New York artist—hooked himself in the nose. It was a ticklish job for me to dissect around the barbs and get the hook out without doing considerable damage. One should always carry in one's kit a pair of wire-cutters, a good sharp scalpel, and a few tubes of novocaine.

* * *

For many successive years the Reverend L.A. Fenwick—known far and wide in Victoria and Carleton counties as "Preacher Fenwick"—ran the Main Southwest Miramichi from the Forks to Boiestown. He was an ardent angler, and it was a privilege as well as instruction to watch him casting. There was no haste either in retrieving his line from the water, nor, until it had completed its curve far behind him, in throwing it forward again. It was as though he had eyes in the back of his head. His fly alighted on the water like a leaf, or a feather wafted by the wind. I am quite certain that had a circle of wood no larger than a silver dollar been anchored on the surface of the water within eighty feet of him, he could have struck it with his fly seven times out of ten.

He was as expert in poling a canoe as in casting. He knew the river as well as he did his Bible; he required no guide. Occasionally he ran the river alone; more often he dropped down to Half Moon Cove, met his nephew (who had come from Fredericton by train) and proceeded with him to Boiestown, fishing the pools not under lease, and tenting on the shore when night fell. He was never in a hurry: hurry was one of the curses of civilization.

When I think of him I am reminded of Jo Davers, Esq., whose lines the gentle Walton quotes with his usual appreciation of the thoughts of a brother angler:

> Let me live harmlessly; and near the brink
> Of Trent or Avon have a dwelling place.

In only one particular did I disagree with Preacher Fenwick: When he had fished a run, or a pool, he refused to go over it again, on the assumption that if a fish were a taking one it would have taken the fly when it had been first presented… Three of my companions fished the Forks Pool one morning. After they had ended I took a brace of twelve-pounders.

For three years, until he died, Preacher Fenwick had a share in our little camp at the Forks. And, for I had never run the river farther than Half Moon, he described it to me several times until I felt that I too knew its various rapids and all the pools; the restful beauty of the enclosing hills... But I had to see it all for myself to fully appreciate the incomparable splendour. For no words—however well chosen—nor any enthusiasm of the narrator, can adequately convey to another what the eye sees and the heart feels.

* * *

It was on the thirtieth of September, nineteen twenty-five, that I began my first memorable trip down the river to Boiestown. (I have made the run several times since then). My guide was as familiar with it as with his own home. We fished a few of the pools until we got to Half Moon where we camped for the night. The next morning—the season for salmon angling being ended—I took down my rod, restored it in its case, and after breakfast we started off. We saw several salmon in the different rapids and pools, but there were other sights more interesting.

Running *Louey Falls* was brief but exciting. Only a few drops of spray dashed into my face as the bow cleaved through the swell caused by the whole force of the river dashing against a huge granite boulder. Then, in a twinkling, we were in the basin and around a sharp bend. Then past *Boyce's Rocks*. How the river turns and twists! Perhaps you who read this remember such places as *The Narrows*; *The Old Hen and Chickens*; *McKeel Brook* and the camping ground below; *Three Mile Rapids*; *Push-An'-Be-Damned*; *Slate Island*—where the Indians, long ago, got the hard red slate to make arrowheads, knives, spearheads, and other artifacts.

And oh!—the glory of the hills and ridges covered from base to summit with a mass of gold, and scarlet, and purple foliage, breath-taking in their splendour. Occasionally we glimpse the Mountain ash or Rowan tree crowned with bunches of ruby-coloured berries; along the shores the now fading flowers of the Joe Pye weed (said to have been called such after an old Indian named Joe Pye); and the dark red leaves of the dogwood with its clusters of red berries.

At times the river ran straight towards some wooded promontory, then made an abrupt turn to left or right disclosing other hills as lofty and beautiful. Often I turned to feast my eyes on one we had just passed. And I wondered that such ravishing scenery could exist, and so few people in the great teeming world (with its crowded streets, raucous noises, and smoke-belching factories) know of this wilderness river, or be privileged to canoe it as we were.

A day off is a day gained, an old woodsman-philosopher said to me many years ago; and on this trip I appreciated more fully than ever before the truth of his words. The pity is that we do not snatch enough of them from the years. It matters not if our day off be beside a wilderness lake or a little river (although I prefer one, or the other, but running water best), or the seashore, or wherever fancy takes us so long as it renews and satisfies our spiritual hunger and helps us the better to face life with its numerous complexities: its joys and its sorrows.

* * *

Most of the guides on the Main Southwest Miramichi are expert canoemen: men who have cut their eye teeth on a setting pole and a paddle. I was glad that I had one of the best. For there are many boiling rapids filled with innumerable projecting granite boulders—in some places as thick as haycocks in a field; and submerged rocks—their heads barely below the surface—that require a quick eye and equally quick work with the setting pole, to snub the rush of the canoe and ease it around them. Also, in places, the river bed is floored with creviced deposits of slate, and I have seen more than one expert canoeman almost come to grief when, dropping his canoe through rapids such as Burnt Hill, or Three Mile, his setting pole caught between rounded rocks or in a slate crevice. Sometimes, by a quick twist he can extricate it, but, to hold on more than a fraction of a second would mean that he would be pulled bodily out of his canoe. On one occasion my guide's setting pole caught and held fast in a cleft of rock on the crest of the last pitch of Burnt Hill Rapids. Quick as a cat he released it, left it there upright, and bending forward seized one of his spare poles. As the bow of the canoe sprang down the declivity of raging foam past a granite boulder, he gave a low chuckle of delight.

Below this, a half mile, we passed another setting pole, its lower end caught in a cleft of rock, its upper length standing straight as a ramrod—symbol of a canoeman's wisdom in abandoning it to the elements. In high water a canoe can be run with a paddle, save in a few places, but when it is low a setting pole is a necessity. The channel is sometimes on the right, again on the left, and these change with such frequency that the progress of the canoe must be snubbed and the width of the river crossed to reach navigable water. This calls for quick decision, coolness, and strength.

I asked my guide if any of his sports ever showed signs of nervousness, to which he answered: "Some of the men; never the women. I had one little woman who squealed with delight running Burnt Hill; and when we were through she urged me to go back and run it again. Of course I had to refuse. We were already three hundred yards below in white water; and I'd have had to carry the canoe overland above the first pitch."

* * *

I thought of that remarkable young French engineer-cartographer, Baptiste Louis Franquelin, who not only mapped the St. Lawrence River, the Great Lakes, and the rivers pouring their tribute into that "Father of Waters" the Mississippi, but also, in 1686, came up the Miramichi in a birch-bark canoe poled by his Indian guides, and was the first white man to map it and its numerous tributaries—including many of the lakes—and record their difficult Indian names.

It must have taken his canoemen a couple of months to make the journey from the mouth of the river to its head-waters—the North, and the South Branches. For the river is so swift that an expert poler cannot make more than twelve miles in any given day—that is until he reaches Half Moon Cove. Doubtless they lived off the forest animals they killed and the fish they speared—a thousandfold more plentiful than now. And yet the physiographic features that surrounded this noble river when the venturesome young cartographer mapped it with such fidelity to its manifold conformations, have changed but little on its upper extent: only a small clearing at long intervals to accommodate an angler's lodge. Were he to visit the river today he would see the angler himself casting patiently over his favourite stretch of water; or occasionally two or three canvas-covered canoes, each with a sportsman and guide, slipping ghostlike around a bend to the mecca dreamed of during the long winter months.

He would not scoff at them for isolating themselves for a couple of weeks in the wilderness. Their contemporaries, unable to understand their addiction to the noble art of angling, might do so.

"You know, gentlemen," says Walton—to his new acquaintances, Venator, and Auceps—"it's an easy thing to scoff at any art or recreation; a little wit mixed with ill-nature, confidence, and malice will do it; but although they often venture boldly, yet they are often caught, even in their own trap, according to that of Lucian, the father of the family of scoffers.

> 'Lucian, well skill'd in scoffing, this has writ;
> Friend, that's your folly, which you think your wit;
> This, you vent oft, void both of wit and fear,
> Meaning another, when yourself you jeer.'"

If you are an angler who read this you will remember the thud of the setting pole on the rocky bottom as your guide suddenly snubbed the downward course of his canoe, swung it hard to left or right of some huge boulder and then allowed it to shoot past—like a race-horse given the gate—while the water swept along the gunwales.

Some years later I was again on the Miramichi. Do you remember, Larry, that day your guide poled you up river from the lower end of Push-An'-Be-Damned rapids to Slate Island? Of course the journey was not as thrilling as when you came down, but you had more time for reflection. For the turbulent water made progress slow—even though your guide was an expert canoe man. It was the fifth of July, and often you were gladdened by the sight of the Large Blue Flag (Iris versicolour), along the shore. And once the bell-like, orange-yellow flower of the Canada Lily nodding on its long stalk. And then—farther on—you caught an odour more enchanting than all the perfumes of Araby, or of any flower that had its birth in formal garden. You asked your guide, Charlie, to push the canoe close to the shore; and when he had done so you grasped the low branch of a birch tree, and held the craft steady against the sloping bank whose crest ended far above you. And then you saw them, each fragile stem—its roots embedded in the green moss—holding up two tiny pink chalices, known locally as the Twin Flower.

And then, as though to add enchantment to the scene, a White-throat loosed his few links of music above the rush of the river—notes that we in Canada love to interpret as: "Oh! Sweet! Sweet! Canada! Canada! Canada!" You told me, later in the day, about the little flowers, and I recognized them from your description as the Linnae on which the great Swedish botanist Linnaeus had bestowed his imperishable name.

It was in the pool above Slate Island that you fished, just before sundown. You had begun casting at the head of the pool. As you lengthened your line and the small Brown Fairy alighted on the water, and the current swung it around on a line with the canoe, there was a flash of silver, a tug that bent your cane rod in a bow of amber, and you were fast to the biggest Atlantic salmon you had ever hooked. The reel screamed as the fish took out line, dashed almost to the opposite shore, then downstream and leaped into the air a good four feet, to fall back and shatter the surface of the water. Then it came straight towards the canoe, and you had to reel in like mad to keep a tight line. But, just as it was a few rods distant, it ran to the left and leaped again. And you heard your guide, Charlie, cry out: "Do it again, you beauty!" And, as though the fish had heard and understood, it repeated its acrobatic feat, then, taking the line over its shoulder, rushed downriver with the speed of a torpedo. You raised your rod high, putting on as much pressure as was possible without breaking the cast, while your guide upped anchor and poled as fast as he could. Past Slate Island the salmon went into the pool below. What a fight you had!

*   *   *

The tents had been pitched below the brook in a tiny clearing used by anglers for fifty years and more; by Indians—both Micmac, and Maliseets—

The Miramichi Continued

who resorted to the Island to get the red slate rock ages before Franquelin had come up the river.

Henry, the cook, was preparing supper over an open fire when we heard your canoe coming back. My guide Bill and I hurried down to the landing place. "What luck?" we chorused.

"Good!" you said.

It was a beauty. Eighteen pounds three ounces; a female fish as bright as a newly minted silver coin.

After the congratulations we returned to the camp ground. Henry had cooked the bacon and was now busy frying a panful of trout we had caught that morning. And I said (of course, Larry, you haven't forgotten): "It's too bad we haven't something left with which to celebrate your success." And then your guide, Charlie, took us each by an arm and whispered: "Come with me." He led us—wondering at his mysterious manner—back to the tents and to an ancient yellow birch tree, its great roots spread Octopus-like on every side. Then he released us, dropped to his knees, dug away the leaves from between two of the forked roots disclosing a deep hole, and thrusting in his hand and arm as far as his elbow, fumbled a few seconds and drew out a pint bottle of Old Parr whiskey. A broad smile wreathed his face as he rose to his feet and said: "Last summer a couple of sports had too much for their own comfort—and mine, so I decided I'd act the part of liquor control agent, and cached two bottles in my bar—oh, yes, there's another: ne-plus-ulcer,[B] or something like that... That's the reason I suggested comin' up here today." And with a merry laugh he led the way back to the tents.

* * *

Needless to remind you that we all, save Bill (who had lately got religion), did justice to old man Parr's memory, and at the same time celebrated your good luck with appropriate toasts. Poor Bill raised a hand in salute. His will-power was magnificent, for he dearly loved a drink. Afterwards we sat down and had our bacon and trout, and potatoes boiled in their jackets, and bread and cheese, and store cookies we had bought at Juniper before we

---

B Of course Charlie should have said *Ne-plus-ultra*.

began our trip—and cups of strong tea. None of "the miserable tea bags" for you, Henry. You threw a generous handful of the loose leaves into the tin boiling kettle, which you held over the fire until one could count three. You said: "Tea is jest right when's it's strong enough to float a board nail. It puts linin' in your stomach."

* * *

No meal in the swankiest restaurant or hotel in all the world can compare in enjoyment to that eaten beside a camp fire in the wilderness with a brook or a little river chanting its age-old music. True, you have no waiters in immaculate white shirts and pressed jackets; no silverware, fragile glasses and expensive china; no printed bill of fare listing a couple of dozen different foods and imported wines and liqueurs. Nor a hundred tables at which are seated other guests—not one of whom you know. There you are a stranger. You are as much alone—spiritually—as you would be on a desert island. In the wilderness you sit on the ground, or on wooden benches ranged on either side of a table of weathered boards, shared alike by your brother anglers and the guides. For all are brothers at such banquets. Henry sits at the end of the table nearest the fire, so that if you want another cup of tea or coffee, he can supply it steaming hot from the boiling kettle.

Your dining-room, which is all out doors, contains pictures no artist can rival: white birches; the unimpassioned evergreens; and instead of an orchestra strumming the latest jazz you have the symphonic murmur of the river, while occasionally a Song Sparrow looses his flawless notes of praise: "Spheral!—Spheral!—Oh!—Holy!—Holy!—Sweet!" as John Burroughs[14] has interpreted it... Or Nicholas Denys's little bird—the Veery or Wilson's Thrush, reiterates his plaintive: "Ta-né-li-ain-Nicolo-Denys-Denys?" (Where are you going, Nicholas Denys?)

Perhaps you who read this are familiar with the Micmac Indian legend about the old Acadian *seigneur*, Nicholas Denys and the Veery—of how he

---

14 "John Burroughs (1837–1921), an American naturalist and nature essayist, active in the U.S. conservation movement. http://en.wikipedia.org/wiki/John_Burroughs

travelled so many times through the wilderness to track for furs with his Micmac friends, that even the birds got to know him; and the little Veery, who had learned the Micmac dialect, got to recognize Denys, and asked him, in words strung to music, where he was going. And, according to the Micmac, they taught it to their young. And even today—although three hundred years have passed—you can still hear it over all this land of Acadia, sifting through the silence: "Ta-né-li-ain-Nicolo-Denys-Denys?"

* * *

We spent a never-to-be-forgotten first night at Slate Island Brook. We freshened up the campfire with birch logs. The stars were thick, shining like jewels between the foliage of the trees that environed our camping place. The full moon rose over the hills; slowly threaded the branches of an enormous pine; stood poised a few moments on its topmost pinnacle, then slipped off into space. It lighted up the shore-line with its trees and shrubs; it silvered the river; it danced in endless rhythm over the waves.

We sat about the fire and talked. Occasionally a salmon leaped in the pool below. Once we heard the loud splash of a beaver's tail in warning to its kindred. Other than these there were no sounds. All was peaceful, enchanting, mysterious.

We smoked our pipes. Our talk was mostly about fishing and hunting. No one mentioned his business, nor his profession, nor wondered whether the price of stocks and bonds had fallen or risen; nor did we talk of politics; nor of the war that was racking most of the known world. We might have been inhabitants of another planet.

Bill thought he preferred hunting: following on the trail of some wily buck over the hardwood ridges. He enjoyed the odour of the fallen leaves, the sudden whirr of wings as a flock of partridge took flight. In the days before the New Brunswick Government put a ban on moose hunting, he got a great thrill at the raucous grunt of a bull, the sound of its antlers against the trees as it responded to the seductive call of the cow—whose notes Bill simulated with such faithfulness through his horn of winter birch-bark. Oh, yes; he agreed that salmon fishing also had its thrills, but—

Six Salmon Rivers and Another

Henry had never fly-fished in his life. He liked to fish a brook armed with an alder pole, a strong line, hook baited with a fat angle-worm, and catch enough trout to make a good meal. As for salmon fishing; it was too monotonous casting and casting a fly over fish that, if one did occasionally take there were scores of others that refused to rise to the most attractive lure—no matter how long you put it over them. "It's clean aggravatin'," he said. "I'd like to sink a spear into them. Nothin' like a spear to wake 'em up. 'Course it takes skill to stand in the bow of a canoe an' pick out your salmon from a raging current. Illegal—? Of course. But I've done it. But that was long ago. Now the wardens are too sharp—too much on the job. At any rate, my bizness is to cook; and it don't matter if it's salmon, trout, or deer steak, s'long's my sports is satisfied."

Good old Henry. I can testify that you did your job well—especially the bacon: never under-done; never one rasher of the panful burned, but just to the left of crisp. You never attempted to cook it over a blazing fire. You raked the coals forward in a suitable pile, and held your frying-pan—its handle wired in a cleft stick—over the reddened embers. I can smell the odour of it as you carefully turned it over. Yes, frying bacon was a ritual with you.

Charles Lamb devotes a whole chapter to his dissertation on roast pig. But, Henry, I would not exchange one panful of your fried bacon for all the roast pig that followed its discovery by Bo-Bo, son of Hoti.[15] And I forgive you the few salmon you took with a spear—when the wardens were far distant.

Like so many New Brunswick guides and woodsmen, Bill and Henry had enlisted at the outbreak of the First Great World War. Henry had served a good deal of the time as a sharpshooter and since he could hit a running buck nine times out of ten, he accounted for so many of the enemy that his name became almost a legend among the corps. Bill had been a machine-gunner and was wounded at Vimy Ridge during the great March offensive of the Germans.

---

15   Charles Lamb, "A Dissertation upon Roast Pig," *Essays of Elia*, 1823.

The Miramichi Continued

Before beginning our trip I had written Henry—whom I had previously met on the upper reaches of the river—told him how long we would be staying, and asked him to purchase whatever supplies we should need.

* * *

We usually stopped two or three days at each selected campsite, and on these occasions Henry had plenty of time to supplement his regular purchases with what he called *home cookin'*. One of his specials was bread. He would mix flour, a little soda, salt, a very little cream-of-tartar and water, knead the dough thoroughly, then place it in a frying-pan and bake it over the coals. Once he gave us bread he called *mul-qua-pun* (its Indian name). He cut and peeled several sample twigs the thickness of his thumb, rolled some of the dough around the upper end of each stick, then thrust the opposite ends into the ground in front of his fire, turning them occasionally until the *mul-qua-pun* was a seal-brown colour. Never have I tasted such bread; the crust was delicious. Several times he served us pork and beans cooked in a baker-sheet in a little tin oven. How crisp the top layer! and the pork, half lean, half fat, was ambrosia. Then, one afternoon, he dug a deep, wide hole in the earth and made a fire in it. No need for me to ask him what it was, or of his intention. It was a bean-hole. He kept the fire going for a couple of hours, then shovelled out most of the embers and ashes. Now he put into it his iron pot filled with beans and a suitable amount of salt pork, then, putting on the cover, shovelled back on top of it all the coals and hot ashes and covered the whole with earth. The following morning we had bean-hole baked beans. And what beans! No chef in all the world could cook any to compare with them. And flapjacks of real New Brunswick buckwheat meal made into a batter with canned milk, and then fried a beautiful golden brown. Then covered with butter, and lastly with maple syrup—that evaporated nectar which Gluskap, the friend and divinity of the northeastern Indians, taught them how to make long ages past. But I think I liked best the flapjacks covered with juicy baked beans. So did Bill.

What appealed to us about Henry—apart from his excellent cooking—was his cheerfulness, his eagerness to please, the smile on his face when we praised his cooking, about which he went quietly save for an occasional song, sung in a low voice. We loved him.

Charlie was a tall, raw-boned man, for the most part quiet but wholly good-natured; a splendid guide, and one of the most expert axe-men I have ever known. Give him an axe and a good hunting knife, or a crooked knife, and he would build almost anything.

Bill was stockily built, broad of chest, pleasant faced, with a smile that would disarm the guardian angel of the Pearly Gates. He was loquacious, and had a fund of quaint yarns that were never dull or boring. You never knew what sort of tale he would next spin. But you could always be assured of original entertainment.

* * *

And that night, Larry—after our two guides, and Henry, had spoken of the sport they liked best, you said (I think the following are almost your exact words): "If we all thought alike it would be a dull world; and if everyone preferred fishing and hunting to other sports, the rivers and the woods would be overrun with hunters and anglers. For your part—although you conceded that every man had the right to choose his own form of recreation—you preferred fishing." And then you went on, addressing yourself particularly to me: "You remember what Piscator said to Venator?—'Indeed, my good scholar, we may say of angling, as Dr. Boteler said of strawberries, "Doubtless God could have made a better berry, but doubtless God never did.' And so, if I may be the judge, God never did make a more calm, quiet, innocent recreation than angling."[16]

I agreed with your quotation from the gentle Izaak, as did Charlie. Bill still clung to his preference for hunting. And Henry said: "Strawberries is all right, but I like blueberries best—'specially when I've made a pie of 'em."

"You know," said Bill, "there's a lot of gooks runnin' round loose in the woods, carryin' rifles, that ought to be in kindergartens, or locked up in

---

16 In *The Compleat Angler*.

cages an' showed at country fairs, with a ticket on 'em warnin' people not to go too handy. Then take all the wild animiles back to the woods an' let 'em loose; 'cause *they* ain't the ones that do harm... Tell me, Charlie," he appealed to your guide, "did you ever shoot a moose, or a deer, that was more'n two hundred yards away from you?"

"I'd say less—often seventy-five; a hundred, or hundred an' twenty-five yards."

"Exactly," said Bill. "An' yet hunters come into the woods after deer armed with enough guns to stock a armoury: high-powered rifles that'll go a couple of miles—if the bullet don't bring up against a tree. No such artillery for me! I've killed more game with an old .38-55 than you could hang up in this clearin'. There was once a feller—" He paused, took a plug of chewing tobacco from his pocket and held it half-way to his mouth quite as though it were a matter of indifference whether he chewed tobacco or received the permission he coveted to continue his story.

"Yes, Bill; a fellow—?" I said.

He restored the tobacco to his pocket. "Well, I'll start at the beginnin'... You remember that New York millionaire woman (he again appealed to Charlie) that had that nice set of camps, at the foot of Push-An'-Be-Damned, that burned down eight or ten years ago—? Well, two falls afore that, when she was huntin' with me up Big Clearwater, she shot a four-hundred-pound bear. Proud of it as a cat with a new batch of kittens. Made me skin it out careful—hide, head an' claws, an' took it all back with her to New York to have it stuffed.

"Well, next first of September, she wrote me she was sendin' Horace up to Boiestown, an' said to be prepared to take him in my canoe to the camp an' look after him good. She'd arrive the last of the month... Horace—I thought—who the heck's he?"

* * *

"Two weeks later the station agent at Boiestown sent me word that Horace had arrived, and would I come an' get him? So I puts on my best suit of clothes an' goes up to meet this Horace—whoever *he* was.

"Well, when I gets there I didn't see any stranger about, so I goes to the agent an' says, 'Where's Mr. Horace?'

"He gives a big laugh, led me to the baggage room, an' pointin' to a crate big enough to hold a elephant, says, 'That's *him*.' Then he showed me a paper that said on it 'Stuffed bear named Horace, addressed to Mr. William Gillalpen, Boiestown, New Brunswick, Canada, Express prepaid.'

"We had a good laugh, then I saw the customs feller, paid the charges, goes back home, changed my clothes, got my horse an' wagon an' returned to the station for Horace. The agent—with some fellers loafin' around—helped me get the crate into the wagon an' I started for home.

"Gosh! I knew I couldn't get that bear an' crate in my canoe, so I ripped off the boards an' took him out. Say, that was a fine job the taxidermist did! Looked as natural as life. Mouth open; big teeth showin'; tongue painted bright red; eyes glowin' like live coals; its forearms outstretched just as if it was goin' to give you a claw. The hind feet was fastened to a dark green board. It stood higher than my head, an' I wondered how in heck I'd ever git it into my canoe—let alone pole it to Push-An'-Be-Damned. I didn't care much about the job when I lugged it down to the canoe; and particular when some of the boys poked fun at me an' hoped I'd get Horace safe to his destination. In fact I had to unscrew the bolts that held the second crossbar, an' take it out so's to accommodate the critter.

"Of course there was nothin' for me to do but start off with my burden, because no one knew better than me that my woman boss was mighty set in her ways. If she wanted Horace in front of her lodge, she'd have him there—spite of hell an' high water. So I picked up my settin' pole an' starts off. I had grub an' some other things—includin' rifle an' axe in the canoe—so what with Horace too it was a heavy load. Some of the boys who were at Big Clearwater (where I stayed one night) made a lot of wisecracks about me polin' a stuffed bear so far up the river; but now I was on the way I took it in good part; particular as I knew I'd get well paid for my work.

"The hardest chore was at Burnt Hill rapids, where I had to unload Horace, tie a rope 'round his middle, then make a couple of loops—like pack straps—put my arms through them, get him on my back an' carry him above all three pitches. Then I returned, got my other dunnage, took that up, went back for my canoe an' portaged it to where I'd left Horace an' the other things. By that time I was quite fagged. However, after a short rest, I started off again.

"It took three days to get to Push-An'-Be-Damned camp (goin' at easy stages) an' when I had finally deposited Horace in front of the Lodge, to the right of the door, I was heartily glad it was all over. But I must say he looked real purty, even though he was such a savage-lookin' beast.

"After I'd cooked some grub an' ate it I went to the guides' cabin, had a smoke, then laid down on my bunk an' fell asleep. But it wasn't a peaceful one. I dreamed of bears all night, an' woke up a dozen times thinkin' I heard a scratchin' at the door. Anyways, I got my rifle an' laid it beside me... You know I don't like to dream of bears. I do, two or three times each year, an' allus somethin' happens shortly afterwards. Either the death of a relative, or friend, or some other calamity... Sort of a kind of forerunner, I cal'ate. At any rate, bein' tired with three days polin', all the luggin', an' the wakeful night, I laid in 'til about eight o'clock."

* * *

"I was just puttin' on my pants when I heard the darndest fusillade of artillery: seemed right outside the door in the campyard. I was afraid to open the door, but finally, I did an' glanced to right an' left. An' there, at the edge of the woods was a feller, in red coat an' cap, who was rammin' cartridges into his gun as fast as he could, an' jackin' 'em out as fast as he reloaded.

"I yelled out, 'Hey—there! What'd you shoot?'

"'A-a-bear!' he stuttered. 'Biggest animal I ever seen out of a zoo. He's down, but I'm not sure quite dead. He was goin' to charge me when—when I fired.'

"'Where is he?' I asked.

"'O-o-ov-er there,' he said, pointin' to the Lodge.

"'Jehosophat! an' the three blind orphans!' I cried—rememberin' my dream—an' started towards the river side of the Lodge, when the feller said: 'Be careful! He might not be quite dead! P'raps I'd better giv'm another bullet.' But I didn't mind him. I felt the worst had happened.

"It had. Horace was lyin' on his side with four holes in his body; his whole lower jaw an' part of the upper shot away, an' only holdin' by a bit of loose skin.

"I turned to the hunter. 'You blasted fool!' I said, 'You've gone an' done it now!'

"'What you mean? What's the matter?' he said, his voice shakin'.

"'Matter enough!' said I. 'You've shot Mrs. J.'s stuffed bear all to hell. Looks like as if a cyclone had struck him.'

"'Good heavens!' he said, his face as red as the sun looks in a forest fire. He come over an' looked at Horace a few moments. Then he added—with a touch of pride I thought—'My rifle certainly did do some execution! Stoke an' Stoke told me, when I bought it, it'd kill a elephant.'

"'Well, you'll pay dear for this,' I said.

"He looked at me a few moments, then put his hand in his pocket an' brought out a roll of bills that'd choke a horse. Hundreds, an' fifties, an' twenties they was. 'How much is the damage?' he says.

"I toted it up in my head as best I could. Finally I said: 'Five hundred bucks, mister; but I can't say that'll quite satisfy Mrs. J. She thought a sight of that bear, an' I canoed it all the way from Boiestown. However, I'll give you a receipt without prejudice. Have you got a card with your name on it?'

"He fumbled in his pocket, drew out a card, an' passed it to me. I looks at it. Name of a Noo York banker I'd heard was come to the river to shoot with Frank Gilks. No doubt Frank was somewhere 'round handy, had heard the cannonadin' an' would soon arrive on the scene.

"The banker—I won't mention his name—peeled off five one-hundred dollar bills an' handed them to me. 'This is for Mrs. J.,' he said. Then handed me another hundred 'This is for yourself; an' I hope you'll not tell my guide what I did.'

"'All right,' I said. 'I'll give Mrs. J. the five hundred. But I can't guarantee that it'll satisfy her. Tell the truth, I don't think she'd have took less than two thousand for that critter.'"

Bill paused, spat reflectively into the fire, then said, "Funny thing about dreams...I knowed that night—first time I woke up—that somethin' was sure to happen. Bears—? *Any* dreams but about *them*!"

We laughed heartily. Then Larry said, "And what was Mrs. J.'s reaction when she arrived?"

"Reaction—?" cried Bill. "You mean explosion an' earthquake rolled into one! She was fit to be tied. Said a swear word or two, then sot down in a chair an' began to cry; regular cloudburst! Finally she grew more calm, an' said to me 'William—' she never called me Bill,—'dig a grave in the front yard, an' bury poor Horace—while I'm asleep.' She wiped another tear or two from her eyes, then added, 'Later, I'll put up a sootable monument.'"

* * *

Thus ended Bill's story. Was it true? At least it had all the earmarks of fact, for although he often indulged in cuss words such as only a Miramichi guide can use without actually appearing to be profane, he had a religious streak inherent in his nature; so much so that he quite frequently sought the penitent bench when evangelists came to Boiestown; and as frequently backslid. As I have earlier said, he had only recently got re-converted; so I am of the opinion that there was a quite big stratum of truth in his narrative. But good as he was at telling a yarn, he often adorned it suitably with some new facet of his imagination. And I'm quite convinced that having once told a story, he firmly believed it had all actually happened, and would have been hurt if you had doubted its veracity. Indeed, Miramichi guides have a rare genius for telling yarns, true, as well as improvised, which would make a quite sizeable *Dungarvon Whooper*,[17] with variations a dozen times.

And *Folk Songs*, and *Come-all-ye's*—No other place in Canada can boast such a treasury as the Miramichi.

---

17 A ghost story, and a song by Michael Whalen, about a murder on the Dungarvon River in central New Brunswick, Canada, in the late 19th century. The name was later given to a train that ran between Fredericton and Newcastle. http://en.wikipedia.org/wiki/Dungarvon_Whooper

Six Salmon Rivers and Another

Henry had a good voice, if we can except a pronounced nasal quality which seems to be a necessary concomitant in singing such songs.

That night we asked him to sing for us. At first he assumed a shy reluctance; but after we had prodded him he said that first he'd like to "ile" his wind-pipe. There was still more than enough Old Man Parr to perform the necessary lubrication, so he had some with an equal amount of cold tea. Then, standing to one side of the campfire, the back-drop of trees behind him, he raised his voice and gave us *Peter Emberley*; perhaps the most famous and best loved song among the lumbermen and guides the length and breadth of the Miramichi:

> My name, 'tis Peter Emberley,
>   As you may understand,
> I was born in Prince Edward's Island,
>   Near by the ocean strand.
>
> In eighteen hundred and eighty-four,
>   When the flowers were a brilliant hue,
> I left my native country
>   My fortune to pursue.
>
> I landed in New Brunswick
>   That lumbering country.
> I hired to work in the lumber woods,
>   On the Sou-west Miramichi.
>
> I hired for to work in the lumber woods,
>   Where they cut the tall spruce down,
> It was loading the sleds from a yard,
>   I received my deathly wound.

The Miramichi Continued

Here's adieu unto my father,
    It was him that drove me here,
I thought it very cruel of him,
    His treatment was severe.

For it is not right to impress a boy,
    Or try to keep him down,
For it oft-times drives him from his home,
    When he is far too young.

Here's adieu unto my greatest friend,
    I mean my mother dear,
She reared a son that fell as quick
    When he left her tender care.

It's little she thought not long ago,
    When she sung a lullaby,
What country I might wander in,
    Or what death I might die.

Here's adieu unto Prince Edward's Isle
    And the isle along the shore,
No more I'll walk its flowery banks,
    Or enjoy a summer's breeze.

No more I'll watch those gallant brigs,
    As they go sailing by,
With their white sails sailing in the wind,
    Far above their canvas high.

> But it's now before I pass away
>   There is one more thing I pray,
> That some good heavenly father
>   Will bless my mouldering grave.
>
> Near by the city of Boiestown,
>   Where my mouldering bones do lay
> Awaiting for my Saviour's call
>   On that great Judgement Day.^C

We heartily applauded Henry's contribution to the evening's entertainment, and insisted that he sing us another ballad. But before he did so, Charlie took his flashlight, and going back to the tents to his subterranean bar, returned with his bottle of Ne-plus-ultra.

After an appropriate interlude necessitated by the introduction of the *ne-plus-ultra* which, if you remember, Charlie called *ne-plus-ulcer*, Henry sang *The Lumberman's Alphabet*. It began thus:

> A's for the Axe, and that you all know,
> B for Boys that can use them also;
> C for the Chopping which now begins,
> And D for the Danger that we do stand in.
>   And how merry are we.
>
> No mortal on earth is so happy as we,
> Tell me hi derry, ho derry, hi derry down,
> Give The Shanty boys whiskey, there's nothin' goes wrong.

C Dr Louise Manny of Newcastle, N.B., who collected several hundred New Brunswick folk-songs for Lord Beaverbrook, says that "The versions of Peter Emberley are as the sands of the sea. It is usually sung to an Irish melody *The Maid of Timarhoe* which dates from the late 1700s. It is based on an earlier song called *Moses Alworth* which, however, ends happily. *Peter Emberley* was written by John Calhoun, of Boiestown. (It was this version that Henry sang.) Miss Manny says that the stanza beginning, "Little did my mother know" is "lifted from the old Scottish ballad of the *Queen's Maries*, or *Mary Hamilton*."

The Miramichi Continued

Then he sang *The Miramichi Fire*, a song relating an event of 1825 of which my grandfather, then twelve years of age, was a witness. (G.F.C.)

> This is the truth, that I now tell you
> For mine eyes in part did see
> What did happen to the people
> On the banks of the Miramichi.
>> And so on to end of the twenty-one stanzas.

After he had finished, Henry—who was now quite wound-up—recited a poem, written by the late Reverend H. A. Cody, Archdeacon of Saint John, immortalizing the Main (or Big Boss) John Glasier who, in early pioneer days, cut masting logs, floated them over the Grand Falls and down the river to Saint John more than two hundred miles distant:

> Don't you hear them coming, tramping down the glen?
> Husky, lusty giants, shades of Glasier's men?
> Can't you hear them shouting, can't you hear them sing,
> Marching on the Squatook in the early spring?
>> Leaders through the dappled dawn,
>>> Warders of the night,
>> Mighty all in girth and brawn,
>>> Devils in a fight.

> Don't you see the "Main John" striding in the lead?
> Clear eyed, strong and fearless, kith of Bluenose breed;
> First to bring a timber drive through the wild Grand Falls,
> First to sight the Squatook lakes where the lone moose calls.
>> Haunter of the silent ways,
>> Spirit of the glen,
>> Dauntless as in olden days
> Glasier leads his men.

Glasier's men are driving, don't you hear them call?
Ghostly shadows gliding through the forest tall;
Inland stream and valley, sweeping plain and hill
Feel again the spirit of the old-time thrill.
    Shogomoc is running wild,
    Tobique's white with foam,
    Once again the mighty drives
    Are sluicing grandly home.

Glasier's men are calling—calling strong today—
From the forest-reaches where they led the way,
Stirring souls of action; lifting visions bright,
Thrilling hearts to daring, nerving arms to might.
    Down the slopes of yesterday,
    Through the throbbing years,
    Comes the message ringing clear
    Of Glasier's pioneers.

* * *

It was midnight when we entered our mosquito-netted tents and got into our sleeping-bags on the mattress of resinous-smelling fir boughs. It had been a wonderful day and evening.

I lay awake for some time watching the stars that threaded the spaces of the foliage far above us, and listening to the rush of the rapids. The owl—called by the Maliseet Indians, *Ko-kak-has*—sent out its weird "Hoo! Hoo!—Hoo!—Hooh!" Far off, back of the tents, a fox yelped. Nearer, a deer emitted a startling series of whistles which gradually faded. Then silence. I thought Larry was sound asleep, but presently he spoke: "Oh, it's good to be here!" and gave a contented sigh.

"Yes," I agreed. Then said, "I loaned my copy of Blake's *A Fisherman's Creed* to Doctor Belyea. When he returned it, I found attached to the fly-leaf one of his prescription blanks, on which he had typed what he captioned "A Prologue for and an epitome of *A Fisherman's Creed*.' Want to hear it, Larry?"

"Yes—please."

So I repeated the verse, the author of which my friend had said was unknown:

> "'God, keep some silent places for us still,
> Apart from those where man forever goes;
> Some altars lit by sunset on a hill,
> Or alcove in the canyon wall where grows
> The crystal drop of moisture on the fern,
> Where ancient firs bend tenderly above;
> For souls of men must sometimes deeply yearn
> For silence such as this to sense Thy love.'"[18]

"How true," said Larry. "It is here in full measure."

A few moments later he said, sleepily, "Good night, Fred."

"Good night, Larry."

Then, with a little chuckle, he added, "I hope Bill doesn't dream of bears tonight—"

* * *

In the morning I fished *Little Push*, taking a twelve-pound salmon and a three-pound sea trout; and Larry, fishing *Big Push*, took a fourteen-pounder. Then, after lunch on the third day, the tents and dunnage once more stowed in the canoes, we began our return voyage downriver. Running Burnt Hill Rapids each of the canoes took in a little water. Bill didn't mind the rapids; he said he wished the whole river was like Burnt Hill. Occasionally he sat down on his seat in the stern, but for the most part stood in his moccasined feet, his stocky figure one with the canoe in all its motions, his broad shoulders slightly stooped as he swung his paddle, or with his setting pole snubbed and eased the craft around a nest of troublesome rocks.

---

18 It is by Grace E. Hall, from a book of poetry titled *Homespun*. Dodd, Mead and Company, 1922. The poem is called "Silent Places". There are 2 more stanzas.

He talked about religion; likened it to his lead anchor, which, when you wanted to stop in a pool and fish, kept the canoe straight with the current. God, he said, was man's anchor. If you trusted in Him, and obeyed His commandments He kept you from swinging with the evil currents of life. He wished life were as easy to navigate as Burnt Hill Rapids; then there would be nothing to it.

His main curse was drink. Oh, no—Our little drinking last night hadn't bothered him. He liked to see men have a good time, if they didn't take too much and get laid out. "No—" he added—"if the Miramichi was runnin' with Old Parr instead of water, I wouldn't drink it when I'm on the wagon."

One of his great fears was of dying while drunk. "I wouldn't like to meet St. Peter in *that* condition," he said. "However, I think I could tell him a good Miramichi fish story—especially about driftin' for salmon (you know he was a net fisherman), an' he'd let me through the gate." After a short silence he said, reflectively: "The Almighty is goin' to have quite a chore on resurrection day collectin' all the bones, an' puttin' flesh on 'em. For example, when I was fourteen years old—I was up to Rocky Bend prowlin' along the shore, an' found an Injun's skull an' a thigh bone. I cal'ate they was Injun's, because there was a stone tomahawk near 'em. Been torn out of the bank by the spring run of ice. I put them in my canoe an' started for home... Just below Calhoun's camps—where the river makes a sharp bend—I run on a rock, my canoe turned over an' bones, paddle, an' settin' pole lost. Only time I ever upset, an' then I was careless—gawkin' round at a fox on the beach. However, I held on to the canoe an' was able to get it to shore farther down, right it, an' dump out the water. Lucky I had my little Marble's axe[19] on my hip. I had to go into the woods an' cut a new settin' pole."

He was silent a few moments, then said: "That's what I meant about it bein' a chore for the Almighty to collect all the bones on the Last Day, 'cause that Injun's skull an' thigh bone is in the bottom of the river several miles from the rest of him."

---

19 Marbles safety axe was, and is, a short-handled axe with a safety guard that folds into the handle when the axe is being used.

The Miramichi Continued

I reminded him that all things are possible with God. He agreed, but stubbornly maintained that fact didn't lessen the magnitude of the task.

He had missed his vocation: had he been better educated he might have written numerous stories.

* * *

A little later, passing an enormous flat-topped granite boulder that abutted against the shore, he told me that it was called Joe Jefferson's Rock. "My father," he said, "used to guide him. He was an actor who came every summer to fish the Miramichi. They used dugout canoes in them days, an' poled up river from Boiestown to a little camp in a small clearin' opposite the big rock. He would get up at daybreak, come out an' climb up on the rock an' watch the sun risin'. Father said he was a fine man; an' often stood in the camp-yard recitin' something about a Rip—Rip—someone…I've forgot the name."

I suggested Van Winkle, and he said, delight in his voice, "That was it."

It was an interesting anecdote about the famous impersonator of Irving's imperishable character.[20] In fancy I could see him, standing on his rock, watching the sun rising above the everlasting hills, while its golden splendour walked the valley-slopes, and lighted up the river where argosies of foam and airy bubbles sailed past him in endless procession and vanished around the distant bend.

* * *

Some time later Bill asked me if I minded if he sang. I said no; not at all.

He had a good baritone voice. His songs were mostly hymns. His favourite one of Billy Sunday's[21] that began something like this:

---

20 Joseph Jefferson (1829-1905), was an American actor…and one of the most famous of all 19th century American comedians…." In 1859 he made a dramatic version of "Rip Van Winkle" and toured with it for many years. He also starred in an 1896 film "Awakening of Rip". Material from http://en.wikipedia.org/wiki/Joseph_Jefferson#Later_years

21 Early 20th-century evangelist and crusader against drink.

> Bright in the corner where you are,
> Bright in the corner where you are;
> Some poor fainting sinner
> You may guide across the bar,
> Right in the corner where you are.

Poor Bill. You had a difficult time holding to the only true anchor. So do we all, although our temptations may not be the same as yours. But, not so conscious of our own transgressions as of those we see and condemn in others, we do not realize the struggle they are going through to conquer them!

We passed Big Clearwater about two hours before dark, ran the rapids at Rocky Bend, then Three Mile Rapids, where our guides had to do some smart snubbing with the setting poles. We went more leisurely through the calmer waters of Pilot Pond and, landing at the Sisters Brook—where there was a little clearing—we camped for the night.

* * *

Next morning we navigated the rapids below the Sisters: those at the mouth of Rocky Brook; and, farther on, landed at the mouth of Fall Brook. Of course, Larry, you remember how—while Henry was boiling the kettle—Bill, and Charlie, led us by a narrow blow-down-obstructed path up the gorge to view the Falls.

While yet some distance away we could hear the mild thunder of the water tumbling over the precipice into the basin below. Then in a very short time we saw one of the most magnificent sights on which our eyes had ever rested. For from a height of one hundred and ten feet the narrow brook—not more than ten feet wide—drops down the perpendicular rock which looks as though it had been chiselled by some prehistoric Vulcan. Great spruce, hemlock and birch fenced it on either side—both below and on the crest—their tops seeming to touch the sky… I have seen the Falls later in the year when the flow of water was much less than now, and spread like a bridal veil in iridescent spray over the rock, and strung with numberless pearls the ferns that had found a precarious foothold on either side of the gorge. It seemed to me that Mother Nature had placed this work of art remote from the river so that only her devotees, clambering over windfalls and slate rock, should behold and be humbled at its magnitude.

On the present occasion we could tarry no longer to observe the wild, picturesque beauty; but I do remember it was so awe-inspiring that we said few words, and even they sounded hollow and were difficult to hear. Finally, we thanked both Bill and Charlie for suggesting that we view this place, and reluctantly retraced our steps to the river and Henry.

* * *

Lunch over, we again started off, Bill and I well in the lead. Shortly, we turned an elbow of the river and found a canoe anchored in the upper pool at Trout Brook Pond. It contained a lady angler and her guide. Bill called out: "Hullo, Jim," and I wished the lady good luck. She thanked me and said she had just raised a fish; so we gave her a wide berth and passed on. Bill said she was casting as though she had done it before; but criticized her rod; said it looked too light for heavy work. "As for me," he said, "I like a rod with some backbone. An the reel—'course it balances the little rod—but—well, I can't understand why people come to the river armed with such contraptions. Now me—" Thus he went on.

Nearing the upper end of Birch Island, he pulled in to the right hand shore to get a drink of water from a tiny spring fed by a trickle of water from the bank. We both landed. Bill was just about to lift a dipperful from the spring, when he noted a green frog perched at its very edge. He picked it up in one hand and carefully deposited it on a rock a few feet away. Then we each had a drink, after which Bill looked up the river and said: "I cal'ate that woman hooked a fish, an' Charlie an' your friend, an' Henry, stopped to see the fun. How about us hangin' up here until they catch up with us—that suit you?"

I said, certainly, and Bill jerked a forefinger to where the frog sat looking at us with its bulging eyes. "That puts me in mind of an experience I once't had. Want to hear it, or have me keep my mouth shut?" he asked.

"Go ahead, Bill," I said, pulling out my pencil and notebook.

"Goin' to put it in a book?" he asked.

"Sometime—perhaps," I answered.

"I could give you enough to fill two or three… Do you know, Doctor, it's odd how things happen. I mean—if the others had come along, like as not I wouldn't have stopped here for a drink; an' of course I wouldn't have seen that frog an' been reminded to tell you my story… Well, me an' Silas Calhoun (not young Silas; his father it was) was up the Spider Lake Branch of Rocky Brook one late June, spottin' a stand of spruce for the Miramichi Lumber Company. There's a lot of dead waters on the Spider Branch, an' it's an awful place for mosquitoes an' blackflies; but worse for bull frogs. Not little critters like that one back there, but monsters—weigh a pound or two or three each. An' not the kind that sings or whistles. These I'm tellin' you about go 'K'rump! K'rump!' with a sort of boomin' sound at the end. Keep it up all night; fit to wake the dead at Resurrection Day. We was stayin' nights in an old shanty on t'other side of the dead water opposite where we was runnin' the lines, an' we crossed back an' forth on a raft we made out of some cedar rampikes.[22] Anyways, it was almost dark, one evenin', when me an' Silas came outa the woods to where the raft was. We'd just boarded it when Silas hit a bull frog over the head with his pole an' killed it."

Bill paused a moment, then went on: "That was our Waterloo—a judgement, I cal'ate, for killing that frog. At any rate, we hadn't gone only three or four rods when we was surrounded by bull frogs: hundreds an' hundreds of 'em; an' we couldn't make no headway…you wouldn't believe *that*, Doctor?" he questioned eagerly.

I was almost convulsed with laughter, but managed to say: "The history books tell us that when one of the first explorers crossed the Atlantic, there were so many codfish off Newfoundland that they held up the speed of the ships."

"There now!" chortled Bill, "that'll make it easier for you to believe *my* story; 'cause history books don't lie—" (I was not willing to concede this

---

22 A rampike is an upright dead tree, especially one killed by lightning or a forest fire.

point, but didn't say so) and he went on—"Well, there must have been a frog convention—sort of political rally that night, 'cause I couldn't ever have thought possible there'd be so many right in one place at one time. An' the croakin' an' boomin'—all of 'em at once't—was like hundreds of bass drums. Well, there we was, an' to make matters worse, Silas's pole stuck in the mud, an' he give it such a yank it broke off in the middle; an' there we was, marooned among an island of frogs, an' the mosquitos flying 'round our faces between bites. Shipwrecked sailors couldn't have been in a worse fix than we was. We filled our pipes, thinkin' that the smoke would drive away the flies. I had no matches left, an just as Silas was takin' his from his pocket they slipped out of his hand into the dead water. I could barely hear his swear words for the infernal bellowin' of the frogs. Finally, he says: 'How about singin', Bill—' cause if this keeps up I'll go off my buzzer.'

"I said: 'All right, Silas. P'raps you got something there. What'll it be?"

"He suggested *The Miramichi Fire* (it's twenty-one verses). So I began, an' he joined in. But Silas never could carry a tune, an' was always a word or two behind, or ahead of me. At any rate, you know them bull frogs stopped to listen—just as perlite as at a church meetin'.

"But as soon as we'd finished they hit it up worse'n ever. 'Oh, my God!' says Silas, 'this is awful! How about *The Lumberman's Alphabet?*' So we started that. An', would you believe it, them frogs was as quiet an' respectful as could be. An' even after we'd finished that song they was quiet fer a minute or so.

"Silas says: 'I guess that got 'em, Bill.' An' I thought so too, but presently they started up their 'Krump! Krump! Boom!' You know, Doctor, even if I hadn't believed it before—that the Israelites made the walls of Jericho tumble down by all of 'em blowin' trumpets at once't, I'd have had to after hearin' them bull frogs; 'cause when they got tuned up proper they made the air shake worse'n thunder.

"The moon came up an' we could see 'em spread out on all sides of the raft. Silas said he wished he had a stick of dynamite—but I said that'd be no good 'cause we had no matches. So it seemed the only thing we could do to keep 'em quiet was for us to keep on singin'. Silas said his throat was about cracked, but he'd try. So we sang *Peter Emberley*. It was twelve verses, 'an wrote by John Calhoun of Boiestown. No relation of Silas—unless it was away back in the time of Robert Bruce (not the Robert Bruce that lives on Bloomfield Ridge. I mean the feller in the story-book who was king of Scotland). Then we sang *The Blue Bird*, an' then *Peelhead*. An' then Silas's throat give out. So I sang *The Home Brew Song*: twenty verses it is. Silas said it made him dry as a covered bridge. Well, after singin' *The Dungarvon Whooper* I give out too.

"An' then the frogs boomed it up again. First one old grandfather would croak, then they'd all start up, just like a band all playin' bass drums. Silas thought a prayer might work, but it would have to be said out loud so's the frogs would hear. (He didn't have the faith in silent prayer that I had.) 'You do it,' he said in a hoarse whisper.

"So to please him I began. My, it's wonderful what the human voice can do! I hadn't prayed more'n a few moments than they stopped croakin', an' was just as reverent as any church gatherin'. But just as soon as I stopped they started in again worse'n ever.

"'Keep it up,' wheezed Silas. So I began all over, an' added some more to it. Well, Doctor, so long's we prayed an' sang, it kept 'em quiet. But human endurance has its limit, an' at last my voice played out too.

"So I said to Silas: 'You pray!' He said he wasn't religious like I was, an' how he wished he'd gone to church more, but he'd try. Howsomever, he didn't do much of a job, not havin' had much practice since his mother taught him his down-I-lay-me's.

"Finally he said he'd have to give up, an' after a bit he laid himself down on the raft. But he couldn't sleep on account of the mosquitoes; an' whenever he moved the water came up between the logs an' soaked the back of him. I sat down an' fought off the flies as best I could. An' all the time the frogs kept up their cussed boomin'. The more sleepy I got it seemed the louder they bellered.

"But just as the sun rose they stopped like magic—same as when you turn off a radio button—an' swam away among the reeds an' lily pads at the edge of the dead water. Then a stiff breeze came up an' blowed us across to where the shanty was. We staggered up the path, opened the door, went in an' made a smudge to smoke out the mosquitoes. Then we each took a teaspoonful of Minard's liniment an' molasses. It's good for sore throats an' about everything else—or so the label says—an' crawled into a bunk an' slept all that day, an' until next mornin.'

"An' that's that," said Bill. Then added: "That experience taught Silas never to kill a bull frog, or any other little critter that can't fight back—likewise with fists—though I admit them frogs made up for lack of 'em as I've told you."

I had been trying so hard to keep from going into gales of laughter during Bill's recital that my jaws were aching; now I let myself go. Finally, when I had sobered down, I assured him that, although I had never seen so many frogs at one time as he had described, I had more than once been kept awake by their croakings at Ayers Lake, in my own part of the province. "As for Minard's Liniment," I added, "wasn't that a stiff dose you and Silas took?"

"Not with molasses,' he said; "it cuts the burn. But it's good fer faints too... You know, I've already told you I like drink too much. Well, two falls ago I was hankerin' to go to Boiestown for a bottle. 'Course my woman—Mary—she knew the symptoms, an' every time I'd think of startin' off she'd faint. That'd scare me stiff, an' I'd put off for a time. But that didn't cure the thirst. Well, one day I decided I couldn't put off no longer, so I said: 'Mary, I'm goin' to Boiestown. There's some things I need.' I gets my hat an' was just about to go out the door when I hears a thump on the floor, an' there she was stretched out flat. Gosh—there wasn't a drop of cold water in the pail, an' the spring a hundred feet away! So I jumps for the liniment bottle that we always keep on the shelf, draws the cork, kneels down beside her an' puts the mouth of the bottle to her nose. My hand was shakin' so some of the liniment poured out on her upper lip next her nose.

"Say, it acted like magic. She sprung to her feet as if she'd been stuck with a pin, sputterin' an' wipin' her nose. Then, when she'd got her breath, she said: 'Willie, are you crazy?' I said no; I was only tryin' to bring her to.

"'Well,' she said, 'you've done it! Now you won't go to Boiestown, will you, Willie?'

"'No,' I said. 'No, Mary, I won't...' Well, a week later an evangelist came to Boiestown, an' I got religion again.

"One evenin', two months after that, as we was sittin' in the kitchen, she says to me: 'Willie,' she says, 'there's been something on my conscience for a long time, an' I have a confession to make.'

"'Confession?' I says.

"'Yes, Willie, I've been a wicked woman; an'—Yes, Willie, I allowed the devil to enter my heart an—'

"At this I began to get hot all over. Says I: 'Was it before we was married, or after?'

"'Oh, Willie,' she says, "it was after. If it was before I wouldn't be botherin' tellin'. I—'

"'What was his name, Mary?' I asked; an' looked up at my rifle hangin' over the door.

"She was always quick witted, an' knowed my thoughts right off. 'Oh, Willie,' she says, 'not that! Oh, no! it was about the faintin'. They wasn't real. They was faked so you wouldn't go to Boiestown after the drink. Please forgive me.'

"Well, Doctor, that was easy. But my story goes to show that we've all of us got devil-awful-suspicious minds, thinkin' the worst of even those we love most."

How much longer he would have gone on had not the other canoes appeared in sight I know not. He had a Wildeian facility of piling yarn upon yarn that was astonishing. As I have said previous, I do not believe that they were made up out of whole cloth—but, like Falstaff, he was not above "adding such embellishments and circumstances as he well knew how." At the same time, like most of the old folk-lore tales, there was always a point, or moral, to his yarns.

* * *

As the canoes came in close, Larry said: "The lady had a fish on, so we stopped to see the fun."

"An' it was," said Charlie. "It was a big fellow, an' tied that four-ounce rod in a bow-knot half a dozen times. At last the second joint broke off close to the ferrule, an' she lost her salmon. Jim—her guide—looked disgusted; but

The Miramichi Continued

he only said: quietlike, 'Now, Mrs. B.—we'll use a rod that's a little heavier, an' a reel that's got some drag.'"

I was sorry she had lost the salmon and, like Bill, I cannot understand anglers using such light tackle... Yet I have seen them using eight, or ten ounce rods, and reels with *little* drag, with the result that they have often had to play the fish a couple of hours, and often lost it. A rod is no better than the reel one uses; and personally, I would rather have a *light rod* with a *good reel*, than a heavy rod with a *poor* one.

* * *

Bill and I decided to follow in the rear of the other two canoes. There is always something fascinating in watching those ahead of you; the guides, for the most part, standing up, now snubbing, now allowing their light craft to glide down some narrow channel. They look so small, so inadequate for their intended purpose, with the waves often running within a few inches of the gunwales. For this—the most extraordinary river I have ever run—is always (even the so-called ponds) downhill—downhill. You see the canoes ahead going straight for some jagged promontory, then gradually disappear—as though they have entered some subterranean waterway—and are lost to view until you yourself thread the tortuous channel around the hidden bend, and see them in the distance; hurried along not by the guides, but by the swift current—the boiling, exciting rapids.

Unlike a journey by motor car—or even an ocean voyage when (unless there be a storm) for days on end there is the same dreary monotony—a canoe trip down the Miramichi is a series of thrills, of new enchantments. You barely have time to catch your breath before you are shooting yet another rapid just as thrilling—or more so—than the last.*(9b)*

The trees come down the mountain-sides to the water's edge or the rock-strewn beach: the ever-present alders, ash, maple, spruce, fir, and pine; yellow, and white birches, and poplars. There are flowers along the shores: clumps of late violets and marigolds, and bluebells among the rocks, and wild roses, and ferns of many varieties. The scents of fir balsam and spruce gum, the indescribable odours of the ferns, all blend to fill the air of this ageless sanctuary with bewitching incense.

Six Salmon Rivers and Another

A dragon-fly (the Devil's Darning Needle, which as a child I feared because I had been told it would sew up my mouth if I told lies) persists in darting about the canoe. It alights on the gunwale within reach of my hand. Its eyes are like tiny beads of gold. Its iridescent wings are like woven threads of gossamer which—with its brilliantly coloured body—reflect all the colours of the rainbow. Does it like companionship, or does it wish only a free ride?

An owl floats low over the river to the opposite shore. No wonder the Indians call it the "silent one", for you hear no swish of wings. A kingfisher drops like a plummet from a leaning cedar into the water after a small fish; a woodpecker awakes staccato echoes as it hammers at the trunk of a dead tree; a porcupine waddles awkwardly along the shore ahead of us, climbs the bank and disappears. A bear swims the river just above the distant bend. Occasionally we hear the song of a white-throat, a song sparrow, or a veery. A flock of young shelldrakes, led by their mother, scurry with paddling feet and flapping, immature wings down the left hand shore, beating the water into innumerable bubbles. In a few moments, having hidden her brood among the sedge grass, the hen bird—her subterfuge not yet complete—flies up the shore past us, as much as to say: "Follow me!" What language does the hen partridge speak to her fledglings? And the cow moose when she hides her young?—and all—remain until they are called for!... We see tiny parr leaping out of the riffles after a hatch of flies; occasionally a sea trout, or a salmon, hurtles out of the water to fall back with a resounding splash.

It is all so interesting, so primitive, so remote from the usual haunts of men. Thank God!—the terrain bordering the upper reaches of this river is too rugged to ever tempt the plough; and only fire, or the woodsman's axe, can destroy the trees. But even so Nature will soon—in half the lifetime of a man—repair the damage; and then this silent place will once more attract the seeker after tranquillity and heartease—if only for a few days each year. For here, if any place on earth, one may find an anodyne for care which equals that nepenthes (the magic potion of which Homer speaks) which made people forget their woes. And Milton in his *Comus* says:

> That nepenthes which the wife of Thone
> In Egypt gave to Jove-born Helena.

* * *

Our journey is almost over. I wish it were possible to prolong it. I have had a joyous outing all over again writing this—in retrieving memories from a long-since past... For it is my river—my river.

We shot past Perley Calhoun's upper set of camps; we saw an occasional angler casting his fly over likely bits of water. We passed Hayes Bar; the few houses—called Hayesville—on a level bench reclaimed from the wilderness many years ago by hardy, courageous settlers at a time when a canvas-covered canoe was unheard of, and each man had his "dug-out" hollowed from a lordly pine. We threaded a couple of islands; passed Strongbow Island—actually in the form of a bow—at six o'clock passed the mouth of the Taxis River and, almost as quickly as it takes to tell, landed on the beach at Boiestown.

Our never-to-be-forgotten trip was ended. We said goodbye to our guides and Henry and hired a light truck to take us and our canoe to McGivney Junction where we got the Express that runs between Halifax and Montreal.[D]

The conductor kindly stopped his train opposite the lower end of the Salmon Hole, below the Forks. Our canoe was quickly unloaded, and with a clatter of wheels and winking taillights, the train sped off into the darkness. Larry and I dragged the canoe over the grass to the water's edge, put in our effects and were soon poling it up to the Forks. The night was beautiful; the moon lighting up the tall spruces that environed the shores; the water reflecting innumerable stars. A great-horned owl, perched on one of the trees, voiced its protest in a raucous *Ka-hoo-agh*! at the disturbers of its solitude. At the head of the Salmon Hole we could see the wakes made by

---

[D] All this was long ago. Charlie, and Bill, and Henry as so many of my old guides and angling friends—have gone from the river. I have not given their real names... What does it matter? I shall only add this: they were splendid fellows, typical of so many of the guides on the Miramichi, who, whatever they feared in this world, did not fear treacherous rapids, nor the wilderness where so much of their life was spent.

the big fish as they moved to right and left. Below the Bogan a beaver awoke the echoes as, rounding its back as it dove, it struck the water a smashing blow with its paddle-shape tail.

In a few minutes we were in our little camp, had lighted a fire in the stove, made a pot of tea and ate our lunch.

Before we went to our beds we stepped out on the verandah to view the river; for we both felt we could never have enough of it. *(7a-c)*

There it was, of course, just as we had left it, two weeks before—as we had gazed at it hundreds of times—swinging around the bend, and gurgling against the two big granite boulders where it joins the South Branch, its moonlit surface reflecting the craggy tops of the pines that stand up against the northern horizon…just as it was that memorable day in the year 1686, when Baptiste Louis Franquelin was poled up here by his Micmac canoemen.

* * *

I have been pondering over the future of the Atlantic salmon. It looks dark. For every fish in the rivers today, there were seventy-five when first I fished it. Drift-netting in the off-shore waters and the tidal rivers has increased alarmingly. With each new dam erected for hydro-electric development it is becoming increasingly difficult for the fish to reach their ancient spawning grounds. River pollution from sewage, pulp mills, end products from food processing plants and starch factories, has created another serious problem that, although an antipollution commission (of which the present writer is a member) was set up three years ago to find some means to get rid of the nuisance, it seems no nearer solution than when it was instituted. The pole-propelled canoe once used exclusively by guides and others has on most of our rivers been replaced by long motor-driven craft. And these, rushing up and down narrow streams create a wash that forces innumerable fingerlings and parr up on the beaches; unable to return to their native element they are picked up by crows and foxes.

It is not yet too late to apply remedial measures but we must act quickly else the Atlantic Salmon is doomed to extinction.

— CHAPTER V —

THE SAINT JOHN RIVER

When, in 1524, the Spanish navigator, Estevan Gomez, was commissioned by the Emperor Charles V to explore the coasts of the North Atlantic and endeavour to find a north-west passage that would lead to Cathay, he first reached Newfoundland, then entered the great bay we know as Fundy, and came to the largest river he had yet seen. He named it *Rio de la Buelta* which, translated into English, means the *River of Return*. There can be little doubt that it was the Saint John River. For here, at its mouth, nature had expended all her art to produce one of the most awe-inspiring phenomena to be found anywhere. Having wound its devious course for four hundred and fifty miles and collected numerous tributaries—some reaching almost to the St. Lawrence—the accumulated waters finally rush between huge limestone palisades (now spanned by the Suspension bridge) and contend twice each day with the high tides of Fundy; so that part of the day the river rushes to the sea in a series of dangerous whirlpools and rapids, then is forced backward with equal velocity to produce what we know as the Reversing Falls. In all, the river and its tributaries drain an estimated area of twenty-four thousand square miles.

After Gomez we hear nothing more of the *River of Return* until June 24th, 1604, when de Monts and Champlain in their tiny caravel with their motley crews of sailors, gentlemen, priests, Huguenot ministers and soldier mercenaries of the Swiss nation, sailed into the harbour, cast anchor, landed at Sand Point, set up a cross with the fleur-de-lis on it and claimed the country for Henry IV, King of France and Navarre. Since it was St. John's day they named the noble river St. Jean in honour of his birth. Later Champlain mapped the harbour, the falls, the three islands above, and described how to get around the falls by the portage worn from time immemorial by the moccasined feet of the Indians.

The river has since had a most interesting and romantic history but we can be sure that much earlier Basque and Breton fishermen—having visited The Grand Banks—also sailed along the shores of the Bay of Fundy and supplemented their silver harvest of cod and other fish by trucking for furs with the aborigines, who had a palisaded village at the mouth of the Saint John.

Four years after de Monts saw the river two of his men sailed up it a distance of sixty leagues. Lescarbot speaks enthusiastically of its varied charms, of the tall pines and other conifers, and of the numerous fish... So many that while the pot was boiling they took half a dozen.

In 1672 the celebrated Nicholas Denys tells us in his *History of North America*, that when Charles de la Tour had his fort and fur-trading post at the mouth of the Saint John he had a stake net in which he daily took so many fish, including shad, sturgeon, gaspereau and salmon, that they often broke the net. Later, Cadillac[23] went up the river nearly one hundred and fifty leagues in a bark canoe; and in his book, published in 1689, dwells enthusiastically on the many noble trees; the towering pines and stately elms; the butternuts, oaks, and maples; the fertile intervales, and islands; the fish that swarmed in its waters and the game that abounded in its forests. "It must be conceded," he says, "that this is the most beautiful, the most navigable and the most highly favoured river of Acadia."

* * *

---

23   Antoine Laumet de La Mothe, sieur de Cadillac, French explorer.

When Henry David Thoreau ascended the Penobscot River in 1849, his Indian guides told him that by descending the Allegash he could canoe down the Saint John to Medoctec, and by a few insignificant portages and a series of waterways reach the Penobscot, and finally the Indian village from which he had set out on his memorable journey through the wilderness of northern Maine. But Thoreau decided that, since from the mouth of the Allegash the Saint John River passed through partly settled country, he preferred to return by the route he had already taken.

It is to be regretted that the famous author of *Walden* and *The Maine Woods* did not take the advice of his guides, for had he done so the enchanting scenery; the forest-clad hills rising gradually from broad intervals; the gently flowing river rippling over the bars,*(3b/e)* would have evoked in him the same admiration that has stirred the hearts of numerous others before and since his time; and doubtless he would have included his impressions in his book, both enriching it and giving added pleasure to his countless readers. Moreover, after reaching Medoctec he would have followed the route of travel most used by the early Indians between the Penobscot and the Saint John waters. In his day the route was through a country almost wholly wilderness which abounded in game and fur-bearing animals and whose lakes and streams teemed with trout and land-locked salmon.

In fancy I can again see the ice in the St. John crashing to the sea, the spring freshet rushing with a sibilant sound—like wind through dry leaves—along the shores of island and intervale. I vision this mighty river, the longest between the St. Lawrence and the Mississippi, and the most beautiful in North America before the dams at Beechwood and Mactaquac destroyed it for all time! Fed by the swollen currents of myriad brooks and larger tributaries, it is mud-coloured, with an opacity which not even the eye of an osprey could penetrate.

I see, in retrospect, regiments of spruce and fir logs, that once graced the vales and hillsides on the Tobique and other regions, rushing downward on the resistless flood to marshalling booms and pulp mill at the mouth of the St. John. And where once paddle-wheel steamboats—such as the *Bonnie Doon* and the *Reindeer* threaded the channels from Fredericton to the Grand Falls, and split the air with the blasts from their whistles, I again watch hardy rivermen following the tail of the "drive" in long dragon-shape batteaux, and clear stranded logs from the heads of islands and shores of the mainland.

When I saw those logs—shorn of limbs through which the wind once chanted its ancient runes—half drowned in the hurrying flood, I was sad until I remembered that soon, as had happened to others of their kind, they would live again in the printed page, and give us, I hoped, yet other books such as Gibbing's *Lovely Is The Lee*, and *Coming Down The Wye*, and Robert Nathan's *So Love Returns*, and *The Green Leaf*, and poems by new Shelleys and Burns and Keats and Masefields. That upon their surface artists would paint new masterpieces; and architects, with painstaking care, draw designs for yet other libraries and schools; and cathedrals with spires in lace of stone and golden crosses to greet the rising sun. Without which "life would be to begin again and the earth barren!"[24] Thus nothing dies. Out of seeming nothing much remains. Even the leaves of last year's deciduous trees, which cover the floor of the forest, will live again in giving birth to flower, and fern, and other trees. Such too—transformed--we must believe—is our destiny.

* * *

Last night a flock of wild geese sped high over the river, a gray javelin of life vocal with the surety of an awakened northland. And this morning, among the branches of a maple whose red buds seemed to throb in the sunlight, a robin fluted his "Cheery-up! Cheery-up! Cheery-up!" Soon the others: song sparrows, warblers, thrushes, vireos and all the rest will heed the great migration call; and from the black ooze of meadow-pond and swamp those small hibernators, the frogs, will whistle their victorious accompaniment to rejuvenated earth. And in this peaceful backwater of New Brunswick, sandwiched between Nova Scotia and Quebec, and

---

24 William Hazlitt, "On the Works of Hogarth, Etc." in *Lectures on the English Comic Writers*, 1819.

flanked on the west by the State of Maine, the gently sloping hillsides will be robed in green.

But the old river, which de la Galissonière and de Vaudreuil[25] declared to be one of the most important gateways of New France, and tried so hard to hold, no longer tumbles with a song on its lips over the bars and around the heads of its myriad islands. For from Mactaquac to within four miles of Hartland, or a distance of fifty-six miles, it is now a lifeless pond, and no more do salmon and grilse speed up it in their thousands to deposit their golden eggs in the far waters of the Tobique; and what once were gravelly bars in the St. John itself, now covered with noxious silt and pollution. Islands and intervals are now far beneath the headpond; the homes of about three thousand people expropriated and themselves scattered.

Many nights, camping beside the river, I had heard the mellow tones of cow-bells mingling with the varied litanies of living waters—like the summons of a wayside chapel calling man to worship things beautiful and beneficent—heartsease from the disturbing clangour of mundane affairs. A salmon leaped, to fall back with a heavy splash. The moon and the stars rode the heavens; a white-throat, perhaps thinking day had dawned, reiterates its ecstatic "Oh! Sweet! Sweet! Canada! Canada! Canada!"

* * *

Thirty-five miles from Fredericton the Nackawick vents into the Saint John. The river here is wide, with several big boulders, their crests just below the surface. On one occasion I was sitting on the beach with my friend, Doctor Grant, and we counted eight different salmon breaking water at practically the same moment. At only two other pools on this river have I seen so much activity.

One afternoon, fishing from a canoe near the opposite shore, I raised an enormous salmon. It came with a rush that caused every nerve in my body

---

25 The Marquis de La Galissonière, Governor of New France 1747-1749; and the Marquis de Vaudreuil, last Governor of New France.

to tingle, and took the fly. I was so surprised I quickly raised my rod to set the hook (not realizing at that date that, if given the chance, a salmon will invariably hook itself); the cast broke, and the fish sank back into the pool with my Silver Doctor in its mouth. I hope it was not set in its gills, for no matter how small it's a lethal dose.

* * *

There were other interesting things than salmon at the mouth of the Nackawick. In particular the Indian Lookout—an elevation from which you can see far down as well as up the Saint John River. And there's treasure buried there—or so the Nackawickers will tell you. And they believe it. But then there is hardly a headland or an island the length and breadth of the river that doesn't contain chests of gold. So that if all that is reported to be cached at different places were recovered, there would be sufficient to discharge the National debt.

One day, it must have been in 1934—Joe Perry was in my office. At that time he taught in the little country schoolhouse at Lower Southampton, below the mouth of the Nackawick. During the course of our conversation he said: "You've done a lot of digging for Indian relics, but did you ever dig for gold—I mean buried treasure?"

I told him no, and he said: "Well, there's a chest of gold buried on the Indian Lookout. Do you know the place?"

When I had answered yes, he said: "I helped dig for it———"

He hesitated a few moments, then: "You won't believe this story, Doctor, but it's true—every word of it... I had only been teaching at the school a couple of weeks when three young men told me they were going to dig for treasure on the Lookout, and asked me to accompany them. It had to be after midnight on a full moon. The place had been dug before by different parties, but they had always been disturbed by some frightful ghostly visitation and had to leave in a hurry...

"You know, Doctor, at that time I didn't believe in ghosts. I was afraid of nothing—man, or devil, so I laughed at them, and said of course I'd go with them.

"It was just after midnight when we reached the Lookout. We had shovels and a grub-axe to work with, and a lantern which at first we didn't light because the moon made everything as bright as day… It was a weird sort of night. Between the boles of the small growth of trees on the Lookout we could see a low bank of mist, as white as milk, over the Saint John. In the hollow, on our left, the Nackawick rippled and gurgled over its rocky bed. Occasionally the plop of a salmon in the pool at its mouth reached our ears; once, far back of us, the wolfish howl of a dog which Jerry O'Neil whispered to us boded ill for some poor body. Now and then we heard the *baa* of a sheep from the hillside pasture, while the faint tinkle of a cowbell rose and fell on the night air that was as still as death itself. At long intervals, from across the river, came the hum of a motor car (incongruous with the pervading sense of native wildness) and we saw the headlights sweeping the highway with a concentrated path of gold.

"There were a few rocks and roots where we dug, but for the most part it was easy work, and in a very short time we had a hole as big as a molasses puncheon.[26] As it got deeper we took turns getting into it, throwing up the earth to those above, who removed it to one side.

"My companions seldom spoke, and then only in a low voice. I gathered that they were quite nervous, so I began joking them; told them we might dig through to China and find no treasure. As for being disturbed by spirits, or anything else, that was all poppy-cock… They begged me to be quiet, but I joshed them the more.

"Well, it was about half past two when Jerry—who was taking his turn in the hole, shovelling out—whispered that he'd struck rocks and asked for the grub-axe to loosen them. It was passed down to him, and he began picking away, pausing every minute or so to throw up the rocks. Finally, we heard a dull, splintering sound, then Jerry's excited voice: 'I've gone through something that's hollow. This is it, boys!'

---

26 A barrel or cask. A molasses puncheon held about 1200 lb of molasses, according to one source; 70 gallons according to another.

"The rest of us, clustered about the mouth of the hole, dropped to our knees and peered down at Jerry. I admit we were all as excited as he was. 'Light the lantern,' he said, 'so's I can see what I'm doing.'

"Archie Hailes, who was beside me, said: 'All right Jerry,' reached for the lantern, which was behind him, pushed up the little lever that controlled the glass globe, then struck a match. No sooner had he done so than there was the darndest caterwauling I ever heard, and the hole was alive with tom-cats—hundreds of them, and they came in droves up the sides of the Lookout. Jerry gave a yell you could have heard a mile. Then: 'Give me a hand up, for God's sake!' he cried.

"Archie flung the lantern at a dozen big toms. It smashed against a tree and went out. We both of us grabbed a hand of Jerry and pulled him up beside us, then we all ran down the slope of the Lookout, and across the wide field towards the highway. And every step we took we stepped on a yowling cat. They sprang at our legs, clawing at us. One reached my shoulder. I grabbed the fiend by the back, tore its claws loose and flung it from me. It struck Jerry on the back, and he cried out to Saint Peter, Saint Paul, and Saint Anne, to preserve him.

"All of us, save Archie Hailes, had thrown away our shovels, and half-way across the field he laid about him like a veritable Samson, mowing down the cats in swaths of fifty at a time. The din was terrific. I could see the fiends; they were all black, and their eyes glowed like fire-balls.

"We were almost to the fence that separates the field from the highway road when we got another scare that almost turned us inside out. It seems that after the hay cutting, Mr. B. had turned his cattle out to graze on the after-grass. They had been lying down near the fence, and now, hearing us coming, and the yowling of the cats, they jumped to their feet and stampeded past us in all directions. Even an ugly old white bull, that was the terror of the countryside, threw up its tail and with a succession of bellows raced after the cows.

"Suddenly, from Mr. B's house, across the road, came the barking of a dog. And that, Doctor, did for the cats. They vanished like smoke.

"We were so weak we could barely clamber over the fence, then, shoulder to shoulder—for we were still scared stiff—staggered rather than walked along the road to the village."

The schoolteacher paused in his story. I was doubled up with laughter, and the tears running down my cheeks. He said, soberly: "Doctor, I don't blame you for laughing. If before that night you had told me what I've told you I'd have laughed my head off... I've already said that I hadn't believed in spirits, nor feared man nor devils. Now I believe everything—everything!"

A year later I was at Nackawick, and climbing to the top of Indian Lookout I saw the hole. In the bottom—half covered with dead leaves, was a grub-axe; and on the surface, at the base of a white birch tree, a broken lantern chimney.

* * *

I was told by another Nackawicker, William Q., about a golden calf, "which was the size of a new-born critter," possessed almost two hundred years ago by the Maliseet Indians of Medoctec, an ancient village of these people.

According to William Q., the Indians set great store on this golden calf; and when, in July, 1777, they heard that English troops were coming up the river to punish them for espousing the cause of the American rebels—so called—the whole population, numbering some five hundred souls, were persuaded by a Colonel John Allen, from Machias, to accompany him to that New England outpost. So they set off over the five-mile portage to the Eel River—one of the links in the system of waterways used by the Indians from time immemorial. But on the way one of the chiefs—who was carrying the golden calf—decided that it was unwise to take it to Machias; reasoning that their new "father" General George Washington, might confiscate it to melt down into coin to help pay the expenses of his war against King George III. So with one of his warriors he took the calf into the woods flanking the portage, dug a hole, buried it, then rejoined their comrades. Reaching the Eel River the tribe launched their canoes and the whole party proceeded to Eel Lake, and from thence portaged to North Lake. But as they were crossing Grand Lake a storm came up, swamped the chief's canoe, and both he and the only other Indian who knew where the golden calf was buried, were drowned.

William Q. wanted to know if I had a mineral rod. He thought that with the aid of one we could find the golden calf, and, if we did, we'd share and share alike; and I would be able to fish salmon from June to September as long as I lived, and have a considerable amount to leave my heirs.

He was quite disgusted when I told him I was not interested in hunting for gold; although, if he could lead me to a prehistoric Indian campsite where there were plenty of stone implements, I'd be willing to accompany him. But William Q. was as little interested in the artifacts of a vanished past as I was in helping him recover the golden calf.

* * *

Medoctec Flat—where in prehistoric times the Maliseet Indians had their palisaded fort and village, chipped arrowheads of flint and fashioned other stone implements of war and chase; where almost three centuries ago a New England boy, named John Gyles, was a captive slave for six years; where the savage warriors danced the war dance before departing to ravage the villages and homesteads of New England—is now under Mactaquac head-pond.

Stockade and wigwam and warrior are one with the age-old dust, and their descendants scattered. The little chapel, built by the Indians in 1717, while Jean Loyard, S.J., was superintendent of the mission, was dismantled one hundred and sixty years ago, and the bell (sent by Louis XIV to his tawny children) which for many years rang out its summons to worship, was transported to the new Chapel at Ek-pa-hawk, above Fredericton.

Previous to the death of the river, the only evidence of the past were arrowheads and other stone objects occasionally picked up after the autumn ploughing, in the early spring after the snow had left or excavated by the present writer and John McClement, the graveyard alder and hawthorn overgrown, and a tall wooden cross marking the site of the chapel. The Betsy

Rapids opposite were now mute. No salmon leaped to fall back sending up a shower of diamond-spray. Desolation broods over the once lovely scene. Only the encircling hills are the same—silent as of old.

* * *

A few weeks following his capture at Pemaquid in 1689, by the Saint John River Indians, the twelve-year-old John Gyles was taken by his master, accompanied by several other Indians, ten miles north of their ancient stronghold at Medoctec—to the mouth of a tributary of the Saint John called Meduxnekeag,[E] where there was one wigwam.

Doubtless the wigwam was situated near the spot where, two hundred and three years later,[27] another white boy (who at the time knew nothing of the story of the friendless and lonely captive) first fished for salmon with a coarse line tied to a spruce pole, and a big hook baited with the lowly angleworm.

Three decades after John Gyles had been given his liberty and returned to his old home, he wrote of his life among the Saint John River Indians. "At our arrival" (at the mouth of Meduxnekeag), he says, "an old squaw saluted me with a yell, taking me by the hair of the head and one hand, but I was so rude as to break her hold and free myself. She gave me a filthy grin, and the Indians set up a laugh and so it passed over. Here we lived on fish, wild grapes, roots, etc., which was hard living for me."

The foregoing contains the first mention of the Meduxnekeag that has come to us out of the mist of time. Almost half a century was to elapse from the day when John Gyles penned his memoirs before an event occurred that was to bring English civilization to the mouth of the Meduxnekeag. For in the month of May, 1784, Captain Jacob Smith, who had served throughout the American Revolutionary War in General De Lancey's Brigade, canoed up the Saint John with his servants to his grant of seven hundred acres on the south side of the Meduxnekeag, and began cutting down the trees

---

27   1892

E   There are various spellings of this stream. I have given that now in use.

to clear a site for his log house. Then, in 1787, and the year following, he purchased from Michael Penn, and Abraham Garrison, respectively, their one hundred acre lots on the north side of the stream.

Sixteen years later his son, Richard, acquired the adjoining four hundred acres from Lieutenant Adam Allen, and now father and son owned practically all the land on which the town of Woodstock was later built.

Contemporary with Captain Smith's coming, other disbanded soldiers, and their delicately nurtured womenfolk—exiles for conscience sake—struggled up the river to their allotted grants in what was then a wilderness; the only living creatures inhabiting it the Indians, a few Acadian French, and the wild animals. Then others came. The pioneers formed little communities, and in many cases gave the old nostalgic names of their former homes to the new.

* * *

Captain Jacob Smith was a peppery old gentleman. Besides lumbering, he trucked extensively with the Indians for their furs, and they were generally peaceable enough. But one day several of them, under the influence of liquor, entered his cabin and, first insulted, then threatened him with bodily harm. But a man who had fought six years for his king, and, under the gallant Lt.-Colonel Cruger, had helped defend fort Ninety-six against a vastly superior enemy,[28] was not one to be intimidated. Snatching up a handspike, he showered blows on the Indians until they fled in terror. Thereafter Jacob Smith was regarded with fear, not unmixed with admiration, by his tawny-skinned brethren.

He was a great lover of horses, riding them at a furious pace over the rough roads; and it is recorded of him that at the age of eighty-eight he broke a fractious colt to harness.

* * *

---

28 Fort Ninety Six, South Carolina. In 1781 the Rebels besieged 550 Loyalists. Cruger was in charge of De Lancey's Brigade, many of whose members later settled in New Brunswick.

Before the son, Richard, died (1833) he made a will bequeathing to "my dear wife Judith" all his real estate for the term of her natural life. She could sell enough land to pay his just debts and funeral expenses. Of the residue (which was large) she was empowered to make and give such leases as she might think proper; and at her demise the estate was to be divided among his parents, his brothers and sisters.

The good lady, doubtless aggrieved at the terms of the will and determined that her late husband's relatives should not enjoy more than she had been denied, forthwith gave leases for building lots for terms of 999 years!

Only three such numerals are as famous, namely: those of a well-known wine which, although wholly harmless if taken in moderation, is otherwise capable of giving as many headaches as the nine-hundred and ninety-nine years leases have bequeathed to the generations who have succeeded the astute Judith Smith, who, three years following Richard's death, married Captain Frederick Morehouse.

* * *

The site of the village of Grafton, opposite the town of Woodstock, was once covered with lordly pines, and the camping ground of a group of Maliseet Indians. And it is recorded by the early settlers that they were often awakened before dawn by the yells of the half-naked redmen, as with blazing torches they raced in their bark canoes back to their wigwams after spearing salmon in the famous waters adjacent to Grand Bar.

* * *

For many years anglers were taking salmon four or five rods below the east side of the bridge that links the town of Woodstock with the village of Grafton. They rested beside a ledge of rock a short cast from the shore. Then someone fished, and took a salmon from what became known as the Patterson Pool. But not a pool in the strict sense of the word; rather a run between the shore and a sand-bar about one hundred yards out. Here, when the water was high in June and early July was a favourite resting place for salmon. So soon the water near the Woodstock-Grafton bridge was neglected, and a dozen experienced anglers and as many tyros proceeded to fish the Patterson Pool. During the rainy summer of 1959 the river had remained unusually high with the result that some sixty or seventy salmon were taken, and dozens lost due either to poor tackle, lack of skill on the part of the fisherman, or just plain ill luck—the fish not being well hooked.

A highly amusing true story was told me about a young farmer who had never fished save for trout. He went to Patterson's armed with a long bamboo pole, a coarse line and leader, a large fly hook he had purchased in Woodstock, and an old brass reel someone had given him. An angler had just landed a salmon. He eagerly asked what fly he had used, and was told a Silver Doctor. He gazed ruefully at his own drab fly, then, standing his bamboo pole against a tree, he took off the fly and ran up the bank to his home. A few minutes later he returned and held out his fly to the gaze of the other anglers—it was now a silver colour. He had remembered that his mother had a bottle of aluminum paint and had dunked his fly into it.

Of course his brother anglers greeted his metamorphosed fly with laughter; but, not discomposed, he waded into the water to his knees and began casting. The fly fell with a splash and floated beneath the surface downstream. Suddenly a salmon swirled, took that incredible object, and firmly hooked itself. After a brief struggle he stiff-heeled an eleven-pound salmon close to shore where it was gaffed by one of the other anglers.

Most of the aluminum had come off in the salmon's mouth so, after a few moments of thought, our young hero snipped off the hook with his jack-knife and ran up the bank to regarnish it with his mother's paint. It is not recorded that he hooked another salmon that day, but his experience proves that, although an aristocrat, the Atlantic salmon will—when in the mood—take the most astonishing confection thrown at it, whether the angler be a duke or a farmer's lad in blue jeans.

A Frenchman, who was guiding a friend of mine on the Restigouche, said to him, "Do you want to know how to catch salmon?"

"Yes," said my friend. "Tell me."

"Fish for them. Keep your fly in the water," was the terse answer.

The Saint John River

That is a bit of wisdom we could well apply to the Saint John River. Anglers usually congregate at some well-known pool, such as that at Hartland, instead of fishing scores of other places on the river where salmon rest. And there are dozens of such pools that only need to be fished to produce results.

* * *

The pool at Hartland, twelve miles north of Woodstock, was one of the best in New Brunswick for grilse and salmon, the latter going to twenty-two pounds, or better. Here, at the upper end of the town, the Becaguimec—or *Et-la-guim-ek*, as the Indians call it—vents into the Saint John. It is a large stream and its volume of ice-cold water lowers the temperature of the river several degrees, for a distance of four or five hundred yards, and thirty or forty feet out from the shore. And, as though nature had decided to be yet more generous, a cold spring from the highlands east of the town runs underground and finally, a few rods from the river, three hundred yards below the mouth of the Becaguimec, bubbles up in a dozen places from the gently sloping beach and adds its icy quota to the pool.

Although fish were taken here soon after the spring freshet subsided, the best angling was from the first of July to the last of August when the fish found this cooler water in astonishing numbers, and so close in did they lie they could be successfully cast over from the beach, or a few yards out.

A few years ago, in July, there was an unusually heavy run of salmon in the Saint John, and hundreds of the silver beauties had sought the cool waters of the pool, both at the mouth of the *Guimec*—as it is often called—and for several hundred yards below. They began taking shortly after six p.m. Saturday evening. In a short time the shore was lined with anglers. *(3d)* By Sunday night, or in about fifteen hours angling, one hundred and fifty salmon and grilse had been hooked, played, and landed. How many were lost is not recorded, but a large percentage always got away. But I venture to say no pool on the Restigouche, nor any other in the world, has ever produced so many fish in the same length of time.

Six Salmon Rivers and Another

* * *

Hartland is also renowned for possessing the longest covered bridge in the world. Another bridge—of modern construction—has been built a half-mile north as a link in the trans-Canada highway which, pursuing its course from Fredericton on the west side of the river now joins the present highway on the east. This new bridge is, appropriately, named the *Hugh John Flemming Bridge.* Hugh John—as he is affectionately known—was Premier of the Province of New Brunswick. Renowned for his eloquence, for his extraordinary ability in debate, and for his human touch, it is he more than any other who is responsible for opening the eyes of the legislators at Ottawa to the fact that New Brunswick is a vital part of the Dominion of Canada.

Moreover, it was due to Hugh John's shrewd business ability that, during his eight years as Premier, he reduced the provincial debt by some eleven million dollars.

But besides being near the birthplace of Hugh John (he was born almost within throwing distance, at Peel) and possessing the longest covered bridge in the world, Hartland had the most famous salmon pool at its very door.

Not only did outsiders come to enjoy the sport, the lovely little town produced its own quota of ardent anglers. They fished Sundays from early morning until dark, and were targets for both visiting evangelists and local clergy whose joint condemnations failed to convince the "sabbath breakers" of the reality of future torment. But it remained for the NBEPC and the dam at Mactaquac, with its sixty-mile headpond, to accomplish what prayers and anathemas had failed to do. The door was shut. Howls of indignation! So, in September, 1969, the Fisheries Department dumped a few salmon of grilse-age into the pool. In diminished numbers fishing was resumed. A few were caught. But, as someone put it, it was like hooking pet goldfish.

* * *

At the upper end of the village of Bristol the Big Shiktahawk (or Sixtahawk, in the dialect of the Maliseet Indians) mingles its cold waters—as cold and clear as the Guimec—with those of the Saint John.

The Saint John River

A smaller branch, called The Little Hawk, joins the river a few hundred yards below.

This pool is comparatively smooth water, a feature that makes it more difficult to fish with the success that would attend the angler if it were more ripply. For the salmon lie here in astonishing numbers, as I personally know from watching them break water, and from the fact that, drifting in a canoe over its placid surface one day in mid-August, I found the bottom literally flooded with big salmon.

It was their knowledge of the large number of salmon at this place that caused the prehistoric Indians to camp on the intervale between the Big and Little Hawks, no less than the fact that it was the beginning of the portage to the Miramichi waters. Evidently their occupancy covered a long period, for I discovered that its whole length—of some five hundred yards—contained innumerable flint chippings, ashes and fire-stones; and, excavating at one spot, I recovered forty-two stone blades. They had been chipped with consummate skill, and correspond to blades discovered some eighty years ago near the village of Soloutré, in France.

* * *

On one of my diggings at this place I had an unexpected visit by an elderly man who had been a lifelong resident of Bristol. I was on my knees in the trench I had dug, and working down the sides with a hand trowel, when I heard a voice above me say: "If you're digging for gold, you should go across the river to the little plateau above where the ferry used to land. There's treasure there."

I rose to my feet, seated myself on the river side of the trench, and invited him beside me. He sat down. I took out my pipe, and, as I was filling it, said: "I'm not particularly interested in digging for gold. At present I'm searching for Indian relics. Of course they—the Indians—left arrowheads, spearheads, adzes, and other stone objects."

He gave me a pitying look from grey eyes set under heavy thatched brows, then said: "I wish you had been with me the night my friends and I saw the Viking ship."

"Viking ship—?" I questioned. "On this River!" (I thought him cracked.) "When was that?"

"Nineteen-thirteen," he said. "I'll start at the beginning. Nothing like getting the picture clear... Light your pipe. I like the smell of tobacco smoke."

He waited until the pipe was going nicely, then said: "That's better... Well, there were four of us seated in my shop late one night: Sam Bedding, Jim Palmer, Terrence O'Rourke, and myself. Terrence was a young Irish immigrant who worked for John Johnson. Later, he enlisted in the first Canadian contingent, and was killed, poor lad, at Vimy Ridge, in March, 1918.

"We'd been chatting for some time, and finally Terrence said: 'Did any of you fellows ever hear at all that there was treasure buried across the river opposite the mouth of the Shiktahawk?'

"We laughed at him, and he went on in a solemn voice: 'Laugh and be damned to you!... You know that when I first came to this country I worked for old Mr. Glane and his wife. As a young married man he and some others had dug there, and discovered a twenty-foot stone wall set in lime mortar. However, as they continued their digging they saw a lot of men, armed with swords and battle-axes, coming towards them. So Glane and his chums ran from the place and never went back. And none of them ever told of their strange experience to any other man for fear they'd be laughed at for a parcel of superstitious fools. But before he died—years later—Glane told it to his wife; and one night, after she's had a drink or two of gin, she told it to me.'"

* * *

The old gentleman paused a moment, then said: "Want to hear the rest of it?"

"Of course," I said. "I'm greatly interested. Please go on."

"Well," he continued, "you must know that I'd heard several yarns about people digging for buried treasure, and of being scared away by something unnatural; but I always thought they only imagined they saw strange people, or white horses, or what-not. Moreover, it always seemed odd to me that you had to dig after twelve o'clock midnight. However, Terrence, and Sam

Bedding, and Jim Palmer, were determined to go across the river and dig, and just for the fun of it I decided to accompany them.

"It was a moonless night when we crossed in Jim's dugout canoe. We had spades, a pickaxe, and a lantern. We landed at the mouth of the Ferry road, climbed the incline to the little flat terrace, took off our coats, and began digging. Terrence was a great hand with the pick. He loosened the earth and stone rubble, then we'd use the spades to remove it to one side.

"After an hour's work we came on a line of rocks that ran parallel with the river, and lighting the lantern saw we'd uncovered a portion of a wall cemented in lime mortar… 'Didn't I tell you now,' whispered Terrence, in great excitement. Then Sam Bedding said: 'Look here, this reminds me that years ago I heard that an old French fur trader had his post in these parts, and trucked with the Indians of the Saint John River and the Miramichi.' Then added: 'I think, boys, we're digging too close to the wall. Let's extend it farther westwards.' So we did, and finally, going down about seven feet, Jim Palmer's spade struck against wood of some sort. Then Terrence went into the hole, taking the lantern with him, and began picking around the object—whatever it was. He hadn't worked only a few minutes, when those of us above ground heard a sound from across the river we thought was someone spearing salmon in the pool. So we turned to have a look, and saw a Viking ship coming down the Shiktahawk… There was quite a run of water in the Hawk following a heavy rain on the headwaters the night before; otherwise it couldn't have navigated it.

"Frightened—? We couldn't move; just stared at that strange thing; and poor Terrence, in the hole, not knowing what was going on at all.

"The craft was about sixty feet long. A big dragon head—a ball of fire on top of it—projected from the bow; another, with no light, from the stern. We could see everything on the boat which dashed into the Saint John sending out waves three feet high, and came straight towards our shore. There were round shields strung along the gunwales, and we heard the sounds of the oars in the rowlocks as plain as plain; and the men singing an outlandish song not one word we understood. The steersman was a great bearded fellow, with long hair beneath a helmet that had a horn curving upwards on each side; and in his belt (about his middle) were a broadaxe, and a long sword.

"Suddenly we came to life, pulled poor Terrence out of the hole, then ran down the hill, jumped into the dugout, poled downriver along the shore as fast as we could go, crossed just below the Little Hawk, landed, pulled up the boat, and then ran across the flat. Just before we reached the highway I turned and looked back. The Viking ship had her nose close to the Ferry road landing; and by the light on top of the dragon's head I could see the strange men clambering up the hill on the top of which we had lately dug. Then I followed my companions. We never stopped until we reached my store. I unlocked the door; we all went in; I locked and barred it with an iron crowbar, and loaded a couple of shotguns with buckshot. I had a bottle of rum in the safe for emergency cases (I've never been a drinking man) and we each had a good one to steady our nerves...

"We sat and talked until the sun came up, then went home... Yes, I'm convinced there's gold over there, but I wouldn't dig for it again. Nor would Sam, nor Jim... As I told you before, poor Terrence O'Rourke—God rest his soul—was killed at Vimy in 1918." The old man paused a few moments, then: "You say Indians lived on this flat hundreds of years ago? *Who* would believe it!" He glanced at the little pile of flint and quartz chippings I had dug out, and said: "Well—well, good luck to you. But if it's odd-shaped stones you want, you can pick them up anywhere along the beach without digging for them."

He rose to his feet, got out of the trench, and with a genial, "Good luck to you again, sir," began walking across the field.

I watched his sturdy form for a few moments, then resumed my trowelling.

I've heard of many strange people on the Saint John; but Vikings?—Well, perhaps some of Leif Erikson's or Karlsefni's men[29] actually did come up this way during the first decade of the eleventh century.

---

29 Thorfinn Karlsefni (born 980, died after 1007), Icelandic-born leader of an early colonizing expedition to Vinland, which his brother-in-law Leif Eriksson had discovered.

The Saint John River

* * *

Previous to the construction of the Mactaquac dam, salmon reached Beechwood dam in untold numbers, and anglers from near and far hastened to the water below and made phenomenal catches of the silver beauties. In one day more than fifty were taken, and the total for the season must have reached six or seven hundred.

About four thousand were lifted over the dam in huge nets. Before being released they were tagged by fishery employees. But seemingly they didn't like the water of the strange head-pond, or were bewildered at not finding running water, for they sought the outflow. The turbines must have caused a mortality of thirty per cent. But others got through intact, and many were caught, metal tags and all, by the fishermen. Beechwood had closed the door to the Tobique waters!

I have seen as many as fifteen or twenty fishermen fishing one pool on certain rivers. But, although many brothers of the angle don't mind how many are fishing within a few rods of them (or have no other choice), I prefer more privacy, the privilege not only to catch fish but, more important, the freedom for contemplation (which a crowd does not allow—especially if fly hooks are whizzing within a few feet of me); for enjoyment of the scenery, and for occasional conversation with my guide. These can best be achieved on leased waters where one is assigned a pool. Having said this I must, of course, make one exception: I do not mind another angler—if he be my bosom friend—casting in the same pool I am fishing, if he is not too close, nor too far away to hear my words of advice when he hooks a fish: "Don't play him too hard! Try not to let him go over the bar!" And when he has landed it, after a hard fight: "Congratulations, old boy."

* * *

I have known anglers on open water—where it is everyone's privilege to fish—who, when I raised a salmon, left their stand, hastened to within a few yards of me and began casting. One, in particular, after I had hooked a salmon, ran one hundred yards to where I stood and cast his fly directly over my line.

Remembering such unprincipled anglers I am reminded of Oliver Wendell Holmes's *Autocrat of the Breakfast Table* where he says: "One who is born with such congenital incapacity that nothing can ever make a gentleman of him, is entitled, not to our wrath, but to our profoundest sympathy." Of course the good O.W.H. was generalizing, and never had my experience—and that of others. However, in the foregoing instance I told the intruder that I felt quite capable of playing and landing my fish, and suggested that he raise his rod high—so that he would not foul my line—and pass behind and below me.

Happily such cases are rare.

* * *

I have been most fortunate in having well-tried friends both on my angling and hunting trips, as well as on my archaeological expeditions.

Among these was a Maliseet Indian named Noel Moulton. *(9b)* If I wanted conversation he could talk on a variety of subjects. If I were arguing some point he never interrupted, as is the custom of so many white men, but courteously waited until I had finished—then he would express his opinion. He knew without being told when I had had enough talk. All his movements were gentle. He was the most patient angler I have ever known, and to watch him casting a line was a delight. When he helped me to excavate a prehistoric campsite, he worked with care. At the close of the day, when it was time to boil the kettle, he would say, "You sit down; smoke your pipe. I'll get wood, water, and do the cooking."

One September day, we went to open a campsite I had discovered the previous month of May. It was on Wapske flat, or, to give it its full name, *Waps-ke-heg-an*. We were some five hundred yards from the river which makes a big bow before reaching the town of Plaster Rock.

We had uncovered a deposit eight inches below the topsoil, and found some of the usual types of arrowheads and knives. Then we decided to go deeper, and at three feet below the first occupation came on another deposit, where we recovered several double-pointed knives—a quite unusual type.

The Saint John River

While Noel was in the bottom of the wide trench, shovelling out some loose earth, and I was scraping down one side with a hand trowel, a man and a boy came catercorner across the flat. When they got near us they paused, and the man said to me: "What you diggin' for—gold?"

I told him no; explained that we were digging for stone arrowheads, knives, and scrapers, used by the Indians long ago. "Got any?" he asked.

"Yes."

"Show 'em to me?"

"Certainly," and I took a handful out of my little basket and held them before his eyes.

He looked at them a few moments, then said, "There was three fellers come up the river last week. They crossed the river on the bridge down there." (Pointing to the railway bridge.) " *They was huntin' fer gold too.*"

For a little longer the man and boy watched us working. Finally the man said to Noel, "Say, feller, just what do you expect to find down there, anyhow?"

Noel pushed his felt hat back from his brow, spat out some tobacco juice and, leaning on his spade, looked up and said:

"Well, I tell you. My great-great-great-great-great-grandfather he leave my great-great-great-great-great-grandmother 'round here somewhere. I try find her." Then he resumed his work.

The man made no reply. Suddenly he grasped the boy by one arm, and said gruffly, "Come on!"

Noel looked up at me, a twinkle in his dark eyes, and said, "I guess that hold'm, Doc."

A quick wit and a droll sense of humour were both inherent parts of Noel's make-up.

* * *

I had another friend: a white man. When I first saw Russell Boyer he was one of several speakers at a recruiting rally during the early months of the First Great World War. He was then a corporal in a Canadian Scottish battalion. When his turn came to speak he got to his feet with the agility of a panther and, his kilt swinging, came to the front of the platform where he stood for a few moments, looking down at the audience, without saying a word.

He was of medium height, broad shouldered, and, as I was to discover later, with muscles and thews of iron. He wore a short moustache, the ends of which, carefully waxed, curved slightly upwards. When he began to speak his voice was clear, resonant, often impassioned. He made a profound impression, and several young men signed up after the end of the meeting.

I did not see him again until many years had passed when I met him at the home of a mutual friend. During our conversation I learned that he was the same Russell Boyer who had guided Mrs. Fairfax when she caught the big salmon in the Salmon Hole on the Miramichi. Thereafter I saw much of him.

He had spent most of his life either in the woods, or, guiding anglers, or as a fishery warden on the Saint John. He knew every pool, every bar where salmon rest and was one of the best canoemen I ever knew. No man loved the Saint John more than he. During the last five years of his life (after his wife died) he lived during the winter in his home at Victoria Corner, two miles below Hartland; in mid-May he removed some of his effects to the large Island opposite his home, and tented there until mid-October. He had cut out the underbrush for about thirty feet on a twelve-foot-wide terrace, on the east side of the island and here, at one end, he set up his tent. An enormous birch tree flanked the western side of the terrace; a maple almost as big stood opposite. There were other trees and their interlocking branches formed an arbour twelve or fourteen feet above his campsite. *(11b)* Robin Hood and his merry men would have been charmed with this retreat. A steep path led down to the beach and the river; opposite was the railroad track, and beyond, a high wooded hill around which the highway curved to the flat and pursued its way to Hartland. He had dug a trench two feet wide by six long, and a foot deep in the alluvial soil.

This was his fire-hole; across one end he had placed an iron grate he had taken from an old cook stove. His boiling kettle and frying-pans were hung on nails driven into the trunk of the nearby maple tree. A small cupboard brought from home held his provisions and tableware. The table was made of rough boards. His tent, eight by ten, was of heavy, oiled duck; his bed cot with a mattress for his own use; there was also an extra one for visitors.

This, then was Russell's sylvan retreat. He told me he would not exchange it for the finest hotel in the world. Usually he wore a pair of khaki slacks, woollen socks, and low shoes or moccasins. His bare chest, back, face and arms were as brown as those of an Indian. His iron-grey hair was cut short; he generally had a moustache. When he smiled his whole face lighted up and his eyes twinkled.*(11a)* He had the oddest collection of swear words I have ever heard. He read his Bible regularly and could quote passages from it without missing one word. Robert W. Service, Drummond, and Kipling, were three of his heroes. I can see him now, standing beside his campfire, as he recited *The Cremation of Sam McGee*, or *The Devil*, or *The Mary Gloster*, and had memorized dozens of others.

Although Russell lived all summer on his island, he was far from being a recluse. Unlike Thoreau, whose dislike of people seemed more pronounced the older he grew, Russell enjoyed company. He had many visitors, including sportsmen and their guides running the river to Fredericton. Almost every day he crossed the river in his canoe to Victoria to get his mail and to have a chat with some of his friends. He had a Rabelaisian enjoyment of simply being alive, and would have thought some of Thoreau's pronouncements ridiculous.

Once, in answer to my question, Russell said: "Sure, I'm contented. And I don't have to run away from the crowd to have it. I live on my island because I like to be near the water. I have lived on it as boy and man. It's home to me. The little I need I can buy. One of the curses of our civilization is that we want too much, and that much often brings discontent rather than happiness."

He was like Diogenes who, "walking on a day with his friend, to see a country fair; where he saw ribbons and looking glasses and nut-crackers and fiddles and hobby-horses and many other limericks; and having observed them, and all the other finnimbruns that make a complete country fair, he said to his friend, 'Lord, how many things are there in the world of which Diogenes hath no need!'"[30]

---

30 From *The Compleat Angler*.

*   *   *

Many times, breaking away from my office routine, I drove to Victoria and, going down to the river, gave a series of whoops with which he was familiar. The river acted as a carrying vehicle for my voice, as it does for the slap of the beaver's tail, and for the call of the cow moose standing beside it. Soon I would see his sturdy form upright in his canoe as he poled it well upstream along his island shore. *(12)* Then, when he was three or four hundred yards above where I stood, and still along his Island shore, he would discard the setting pole, seize the paddle and, taking advantage of the swift current, strike a diagonal course to the Victoria side of the river.

I particularly remember one such occasion when I stayed all night with him. Shortly after we had reached his retreat he mixed what he called his Vesper Cocktail. Ingredients: plenty of rum, some vermouth, lime juice, and brown sugar which he stirred for fully two minutes. I thought it might be quite potent and suggested that he add some water; at which he said, "Water—? Why Doc, the rum was watered long before it left the Liquor Commission Store." Then, pointing to the river that flowed past his Island, "Talk about our forest being our greatest asset... All wrong... Old Man Saint John's got 'em beat a mile. Now they're talking about building a dam to conserve the flow."

He took a sip of his Vesper Cocktail and said: "Not too bad; but if the rum were 100 per cent proof it'd be better."

I didn't argue the point, but poured two-thirds of mine into an empty glass that stood on the table, saying I'd probably drink it in the morning. Russell, however, protested that the night air would spoil it, and added it to what remained in his own glass; then proceeded to fry his beefsteak which, when done, would have won the approval of the most fastidious gourmet. And in another pan were fried potatoes he had boiled that noon; and in his black boiling kettle brewed tea.

*   *   *

After the dishes had been washed and put away, we sat before the fire and talked. The moon came up over the hills; the stars winked through the canopy of foliage far above the *Retreat*; the river murmured its age-old music over the bar at the lower end of the Island.

"My God!" said Russell with profound reverence in his voice. "Isn't this a peaceful place?... You know, Doc, the Lord God made for us a heaven right here on this planet, placed us in it, and immediately we began to make of it a hell. Think of all the wars during the last two thousand years (not to mention those that raged before); think of the young men—some not more than boys, who have given up their breath on hundreds of battlefields. Why?—Why? I sometimes ask myself. And finally I realize that many have been fought in the name of religion—the religion of Jesus Christ. And many because some petty king (that wouldn't make good bear bait) coveted something his brother king had. And others because silly politicians haven't had the wits, or the will, to steer us into the paths of peace. And so more youths are sacrificed on the fields of battle; and when it's all over we are often in much the same state as we were before. I know. I've read some history. But—let's talk of something more pleasant."

So we talked of the river—his river, for he was a part of it. He not only loved it; he had run it by night as well as by day; he not only knew every bar, rock, and ledge, but, like certain airmen, had the sight of a cat. Once, travelling through the woods with him after dark, before the moon had risen, I bumped against a tree. He took me by the hand and led me to our destination. Poachers on the river feared him. One told me that you'd never hear the approach of his canoe—only his voice: "You'd better come to shore, boys."

* * *

Just as the sun was pushing its disk over the eastern hills Russell got up and, towel over one shoulder, went down to the beach. A few moments later I heard a heavy splash, then grunts and chuckles as he enjoyed himself in the river. I rose and dressed...I had no desire to follow his example.

When he returned to his Retreat he smiled, wished me good morning, then said, "How about a matutinal cocktail?"

"Matutinal—?" I queried. "I never heard of one. Are the makings the same as your Vesper cocktail?"

He gave a low laugh. "Only difference is in the name."

"Well, then, make mine *very* small," I said.

With the barely audible remark that my education had been sadly neglected he said, in a louder voice, that some time I must try his Thunder and Lightning (a drink he had named after a famous salmon fly). It would, he added with a broad smile, make my hair curl. Then he began mixing his matutinal cocktail.

"Just a wee one for me," I reminded him.

He obeyed, then filled his own glass to the brim. He didn't drink it immediately. Turning to me he said: "What a beautiful morning! That sun, the trees, the grasses sparkling with dew, the river journeying to the sea... Smell the pure, scented air? Nothing like it in the cities. I've been in 'em. London, Montreal—when I went with other Canucks to shoot at Bisley.[31] And New York once, from November until mid-March... Why, how many people in Hartland, Woodstock, and other towns are now awake? Not more'n a dozen. The rest won't get up 'till eight o'clock. Know what I'd like to do—?"

Without waiting for my reply he answered his own question: "I'd like to have the magic flute of that Pied Piper I read about years ago in one of my school readers, and march through the streets and wake up all the people—young and old, then lead them to the top of some high hill and tell 'em to gaze on the beauty that God Almighty made for them... No, Doc, people haven't really lived who've never seen a sunrise... Look at the dew sparkling on the grass by that birch tree—"

"Here at thy feet fond dryads string their pearls of lucent dew to make a silver snood—" I quoted from one of my own poems.[32]

"Now, that's a nice thought," commented Russell. "Pearls of dew... Dryads—" He swallowed his matutinal cocktail and went on, "I saw one three years ago (I mean a Dryad)... Sit down, Doc." He pulled a camp stool before the fire on which he threw a few sticks, then he too sat down opposite me.

---

31 The Bisley Shooting Grounds in Woking, Surrey, England.

32 Unpublished; it has not survived among GFC's MSS.

"Hold it, Russell," I said, "I want to get my notebook and pencil. I fancy this is worth taking down." In half a minute I was again seated, and he began where he had left off.

"The fog was hanging low over the river, so I couldn't see her well at first. She was about two hundred yards upstream, her head and face towards the opposite shore… Thought it might be an otter. Then she turned over on her side facing my Island, and I saw her white face and arms. She swam down to the big rock over there, climbed up on it, and sat with her hands clasped about her knees—about a nineteen-year-old, I thought.[F]

"I called out, 'Hullo! Where the Sam Hill did you come from?'

"She couldn't have been more surprised and startled if I'd fired off a cannon. She let her hands drop to the rock, and I thought she was going to jump into the water and disappear. But she didn't. She turned her face to me and I saw it was the most beautiful I'd seen in years. Then she called out in a clear, musical voice. '*Good morning…I swam down from Hartland*'.

"'Holy Mackinaw, and the old Davis Ram!' I said, 'That's two miles! You're not thinking of swimming back?'

"'No,' she answered, with a lovely smile… 'I never heard that one before… There's a road over there, I believe.' And she pointed to the opposite shore.

"'Where's your home?' I asked (for I knew she was a stranger to Hartland.) 'That is,' I added, 'if you don't mind telling me.'

"'Not at all,' said the Dryad. 'I'm from Exeter, New Hampshire. Father motored up here to fish the Hartland Pool, so I came with him… This is a beautiful country. A lovely river.'

"Of course, Doc, I agreed—She'd hit me in one of my soft spots. Then I said, 'Had any breakfast?'

"'Oh no,' she answered. 'I wouldn't think of swimming soon after eating. Besides, I was up before anyone else.'

"'That's right,' I said. 'Look here, Miss—how about coming to shore and having some of my grub—? I'm just about to boil the kettle. I can give you bacon and eggs, toast, and tea—or coffee—whichever you like best.'

F   I suggested to Russell that, since he first saw the maiden in the river, he should have called her a Naiad, but he protested that she was more Dryad because she loved trees.

"She hesitated a moment, then said, 'Would your name be Russell?'

"'None other,' I replied. 'How'd you guess?'

"'Oh,' she said, with a bewitching smile, 'you were at the Pool yesterday. You were so brown I thought you were an Indian, so I asked one of the anglers. He told me about you... Yes, thank you, I'll be very happy to share your breakfast.' She rose to her feet, made a neat dive leaving scarcely a ripple, and coming up swam to where she got footing, straightened, then walked to shore, the water dripping from her bathing suit. Then she removed her cap, gave a shake of her head that loosened her short, chestnut-coloured hair, and gazed at me fearlessly, a little smile in her dark grey eyes. She stood as straight as a birch sapling that has never been bent by wind or storm. Her limbs were perfect and made me think of a doe deer.

"I asked my Dryad if she'd like a towel...I had a fresh one. She said yes. So I ran up the bank, got one and a blanket I'd bought and never used.

"When I got back she gave a low laugh of pleasure, thanked me, and I returned here and started up the fire. A little later she joined me, stood looking about her: at my fire (You know, Doc, how when people first come into a room that has an open fire it's almost the first thing they look at) and exclaimed, 'How nice!' Then at my big birch tree, and my maple with the kettles and frying-pans hung along its trunk; and the space I'd cleared between the alders and white birches. 'Oh,' she cried, 'how perfectly wonderful! It's like a fairy dell. Daddy *must* see this!... It reminds me of *Lavengro*, and *Romany Rye*.'

"'Never drank any rye but Canadian—Royal Crown,' I said.

"She threw back her head and laughed until the tears came to her eyes. Then she said, 'Pardon me...but, oh, this is precious!' Then she told me that *Lavengro* and *Romany Rye* were books written by a man named—Borrow (I think it was) about Gypsies.

"At this I too laughed and she joined in. Her laughter was like a little brook tinkling over its rocky bed.

"Then I got her a camp stool, placed it on one side of the fire and asked her to sit down and enjoy herself. So she did, with my blanket over her shoulders, and warmed her shins, and watched me with her fine eyes as I hung my boiling kettle over the blaze and began frying a panful of bacon.

"That was a wonderful hour. The bacon was done to a turn, and I broke a raw egg into the boiling kettle where I'd put the coffee. She was much interested when I cut a hazel stick with a forked branch, set a slice of bread on it and toasted it over the coals.

"As we ate and talked she said very likely her father was now fishing Hartland Pool… He had never hooked an Atlantic salmon, and was most anxious to get one.

"I told her I hoped he would, but that salmon seldom or never take when the fog is lying low over the water.

"Well, after we'd had breakfast she thanked me, said it was the best meal she'd had in a long time. The coffee was delicious. Then—after a few minutes—she said she'd better be getting back to Hartland, and asked me if I'd mind putting her across to the opposite shore.

"'I'll do better than that,' I said, 'I'll canoe you to Hartland… Get you there in twenty-five minutes. Quicker than you could walk by the road.'

"'Oh,' she said, 'that will be wonderful!' And she gave me a smile that was worth a million dollars.

"And so, after she was seated in the canoe, I stepped in and poled her along the shallow shore water. The fog had lifted, and a short distance from the Pool I saw that someone was playing a salmon.

"'It's Daddy!' she cried excitedly.

"'Well,' I said—as the fish threw a somersault into the air—'it's a big one… Looked like a fifteen-pounder.' Then I put my back and arms to the setting pole, because I wanted her to be in at the kill.

"I landed her below where some other anglers were fishing, then we both of us hurried up the beach to where her father stood, one hand clamped about his rod handle, the other reeling in as fast as he could. His guide stood out in the water with his long-handled net ready for business.

"But when the salmon was within a few feet of him it suddenly swerved and tore like a thunderbolt out of the pool and into the heavy water. The reel screeched: I'd say it almost smoked. The Dryad's father had his rod tip too low, and I couldn't help saying, 'Hold your rod tip up, mister; and cant the butt a little to the right. That'll turn him.'

"He did so. His guide shot me a black look that said, plain as day, what right had I to butt in.

"Well, that pressure on the salmon's mouth did the trick. It turned upriver, and again swung towards shore while the Dryad's father reeled in line like mad. Again in calmer water the salmon rolled over on its side, and floated half lifeless—just beyond and above the guide's submerged net.

"I was standing close to the shoulder of the Dryad's father. Now I said in a low voice, 'Let it drop back…a little more… Not too much pressure… there.' The salmon was over the net. With one quick movement the guide lifted the mass of silver out of the water and came to shore, killed it with a few taps over the head, and then weighed it. Fifteen pounds five ounces. This was before the Mactaquac dam spoiled fishing."[33]

* * *

"I said farewell to my Dryad, who promised she would never forget me. Then I got into my canoe and returned to the Island… But that, Doc, was not the last time I was to see her… Next morning—just a bit after sunrise—I saw her swimming downriver towards my shore. When she landed I saw she had a small knapsack strapped to her shoulders that I later found contained a pair of blue jeans, a light sweater and low moccasins, done up in one of those new-fangled waterproof bags… And can you guess what she'd brought *me*—?"

I shook my head.

Russell's face broadened with a happy grin. "Nor anyone else… Well, it was a quart bottle of *Dewar's Special* her father had sent me. Then she told me she'd like to stay the day—if I didn't mind. That her father would walk down the highway shortly after supper, bringing his rod, and hoped I'd take him out in my canoe while he fished the run on the west side of the Island.

"Of course I was delighted. She asked me if she could use my tent a few minutes while she put on her dry things. I said certainly… Shortly she came out in the jeans, sweater, and moccasins, and helped me cook breakfast.

---

33   Russell died in 1950; he couldn't have said anything about Mactaquac.

She especially wanted to toast the bread over my forked hazel stick. She was like a little girl in her joy of each new discovery.

"After we'd breakfasted and washed the dishes, we sat down and talked. Later I recited *The Cremation of Sam McGee*, and *The Devil*. She liked both; but *The Devil* best—especially where Louis Desjardine gives him a pipe of Canadian tobacco that starts him gasping and yelling for fresh air; and then Louis opens the door, puts the devil on a chair and tosses him outside; and then goes back, lights his pipe and fills the room with tobacco smoke; and how he continues smoking and the devil is too scared to come in... She doubled up over that; and when she'd wiped the tears from her eyes said I should read it over the radio... Then we took a walk to the upper end of the Island where Bill Sommers has a vegetable garden, and got some carrots, cucumbers, and ripe tomatoes. After our return we sat down and talked. She asked me (what you and scores of others have) if I was contented to live on my Island, and if I didn't ever get lonely. I told her I was contented. As for being lonely sometimes—not as much as if I were living in a city. 'A city,' I said, 'is the loneliest place under God's heaven. You often don't know your next-door neighbour. I know. I worked in one six months. Now here I have everything I need. If I hanker after a little sociability I paddle over to Victoria, or go up to the Hartland Pool. Then people come right here to see me—like you—only they don't swim. They walk down the road and give me a whoop. I hear: 'Russ—ell! Russ—ell!' and I go and bring them across... And I have my books. I learn one new poem every week or so and memorize something I like out of the Bible.' Then I said, 'I'm not any saint. Been quite wicked in my day... But no use worrying about the past; concentrate on today and try to be happy.' Then I said, 'Better is a little with righteousness than great revenues without right.' And Proverbs again says, 'How much better it is to get wisdom than gold! and to get understanding rather than to be chosen than silver.' You read Proverbs, miss, and if you take it to heart you can't go far wrong.'

"She nodded, then said what made me know she quite understood: 'You know, Russell, when I was a very little girl, my mother often read me Burgess's *Bed-time Stories*. Tale about animals for children. I think my favourite story was about Johnny Chuck finding the Greatest Thing in the World. All the animals were scurrying through the forest in the effort to find it, but Johnny Chuck stayed home and listened to Mother West Wind talking. And when all the other animals returned, Mother West Wind told them that Johnny Chuck had stayed home and found what they had been looking for—the Greatest Thing in the World. And then one asked her what was the Greatest Thing in the World. And she told them it was *Contentment.*'

"'Now that little story,' I said, 'hits me right in the solar-plexus.'

"Well, Doc—to shorten my story—the Dryad's father came opposite here about six o'clock, and I went over and got him. After he had sampled my Vesper cocktail and rested a bit, we fished the Run while his daughter curled herself up in my blanket and had a nap. He hooked and landed a five-pound grilse; and at the mouth of the spring brook opposite the run lost a big salmon.

"After dark I poled the Dryad and her Dad up to Hartland. It was a wonderful night, the sky thick with stars, and a moon in its first quarter turned the ripples to silver.

"Two days later they departed for New Hampshire. Gosh! that did make me lonely. Like when any lovely things goes out of your life—She sent me a card from some place on the way, again thanking me for my entertainment. The following August I got a long letter dated from Rome (I'll show it to you later) where she'd gone with some other girls. It was filled with the sights she'd seen; the paintings in the Vatican; the pictures in the Marcian Library. She wrote at some length of the gorgeous sunsets; of the bridge of San Christoforo; of San Gregorio…of sailing in a gondola along the lagoons of Venice. (You see, Doc, I remember 'em all because I've read the letter a score of time.) 'But, Russell,' she added, 'your Island—your Saint John River—appealed to me more than anything I've seen or experienced over here. Perhaps it was the serenity of your river, and the simplicity and back-to-earthness of your delightful camping place. While I was there it seemed that I was transported to another planet… Perhaps it was the knowledge that you had found the *Greatest Thing in the World,* and made *me* realize more fully that it is the only thing that really matters. And, Russell, although I have been in the finest restaurants on the Continent, none of the food can compare to the bacon and eggs you cooked for me over your fire-hole, nor have I tasted any coffee as delicious as that you made in your black boiling kettle.'"

Russell paused, then, shaking his grizzled head said: "What a girl!"

"Did you ever see her again?" I asked.

"No. But I had a letter from her last 12th July— You know, Doc, my birthday was on the anniversary of the Battle of the Boyne— She'd asked me, and I told her—She said she and her father were coming to Hartland next year, and she would certainly see me... Yes... She was beautiful... Not your pretty-pretty sort. She had a fine mind, was a good talker but could be silent, too... You know the river and the woods impart their own magic to the true lover of nature."

"'To be beautiful and to be calm, without mental fear, is the ideal of nature,'" I quoted. And added, "Richard Jefferies wrote that."[34]

"I'd like to have known him," said Russell.

* * *

In 1950 Russell was laid to rest in the little cemetery that overlooks the Saint John and the Island he loved so well. When I pass the place I always lift one hand in salute to a man who not only imparted to me his vast knowledge of the river, and the woods and its wild life, but in many other ways proved his love for me.

Often he had repeated for me what he called his favourite toast. He told me he got it from a grizzled old sea captain: a famous rum-runner (who was always accompanied by a ferocious-looking English bulldog) he had first met, and later become friendly with, while walking along the water front at Halifax, Nova Scotia.

If it is copyrighted I sincerely trust that both the author and the publisher will forgive me for including it in this book. For it reveals a part of Russell's philosophy as doubtless it did of the person who wrote it:

---

34   *The Life of the Fields*, 1884.

> Life! we've been long together,
> Through pleasant and through cloudy weather,
> 'Tis hard to part when friends are dear,
> Perhaps 'twill cost a sigh, a tear,
> —Then steal away, give little warning;
> Choose thine own time,
> Say not Goodnight, but in some brighter clime
> Bid me Good Morning, friend,
> —Bid me Good Morning.

Recently I was looking through Palgrave's *Golden Treasury*, and discovered that the lines Russell quoted were written by Anna Letitia Barbauld (1743-1825). But either Russell's rum-running friend chose to shorten the original poem, or else Russell himself did so, but added "friend" to the eighth line, and then repeated "Bid me Good Morning." At any rate the addition of "friend" and the repetition of "Bid me Good Morning" seem to me to make the poem more effective. Russell had a good sense of balance, and, moreover, knew its effectiveness on the mind by repeating a very striking sentence.

The reader can judge from the original poem quoted below:

> "Life! I know not what thou art,
> But know that thou and I must part;
> But when, or how, or where we met
> I own to me's a secret yet.
> Life! we've been long together
> Through pleasant and through cloudy weather;
> 'Tis hard to part when friends are dear—
> Perhaps 'twill cost a sigh, a tear;
> —Then steal away, give little warning,
> Choose thine own time;
> Say not Good Night—but in some brighter clime
> Bid me Good Morning."
>
> (A. L. Barbauld)

— CHAPTER VI —
THE RESTIGOUCHE AND KEDGWICK

If Jacques Cartier, after he had rounded Point Miscou that hot July day in 1534 and explored for a distance of twenty-five leagues the coastline of the beautiful sheet of water he named Baie de Chaleur, had sailed a little farther, he would have entered the mouth of the Restigouche which, with its numerous tributaries that push their crystal-clear fingers into a still untamed wilderness, has for many years lured anglers from near and far to cast their feathered confections over the most elusive and aristocratic of all fish.

Although the Restigouche—which the Micmac Indians call *Lust-a-Gouche* (there is no R in the dialects of the north-eastern Indians) was fly-fished for salmon previous to the 1860s, the first accounts I have found of visiting anglers are those contained in *Chip-lo-quorgan*[G] or *Life by the Campfire*, by Captain Richard Dashwood; and that of a trip up the river in the late summer of 1867, by *Penman*[35] and a Captain of a British gunboat, published in *Harper's New Monthly* for March, 1868. The article by *Penman* (the author's pseudonym) is a superb bit of writing. He had a keen eye for the topographical features of the river and fine feeling for its manifold charms.

---

35 "Penman" (Charles Hallock), "The Restigouche". It can be read online at: http://www.unz.org/Pub/Harpers-1868mar-00424

G It should be *Chip-la-kwa-gan* (a stick to hold a boiling kettle over the fire).

Dashwood arrived at Saint John on March 24th, 1862, with other members of the XVth Imperial regiment, and on the 15th May made a trip to the Schoodic lakes—the source of the St. Croix River of which the centre is the boundary between the Province of New Brunswick and the State of Maine. He says that the St. Croix formerly abounded in salmon, but was then blocked up by dams and quite impassable. He speaks with enthusiasm of the splendid trout fishing. The fish rising so greedily that he continually hooked two at once and the fish broke his casting line by jumping in different directions at the same moment, so that he was obliged to fish with only one fly... He found the trout fishing in the Schoodic lakes the best in North America.

On the first of the following July, Dashwood left Saint John with two brother officers for Bay Chaleur on a salmon fishing expedition. They first fished the Cascapedia, each man in a birchbark canoe with two Micmac guides. The stream was so swift they could make no more than ten miles each day—it took them a week to reach the Forks, a distance of sixty miles from the sea. They caught plenty of sea trout on the way up, some weighing five pounds, and met a settler coming down the river with his canoe half filled with them. Dashwood and his friends took but two salmon at the Forks after several days fishing, and "decided that the river, as regards salmon, was a myth."

In early August, 1863, Dashwood went to the Restigouche, fished five miles up the Matapedia and at two good pools had "fair sport". And says he "was rather late for the best run—which takes place in July." He recounts that "there is good fishing on the Quata-wam-kedgewick, another tributary of the Restigouche," but claims that "the worst of the Restigouche is that the pools are very few, and about thirty miles apart, but the fish are larger than those of any other river of the province."

It would seem that Captain Dashwood's guides must have hurried him along, for there are dozens of splendid pools seldom more than a few rods apart from the head waters of the Kedgwick to its mouth, and for fifty miles down the Restigouche to tide-head.

* * *

Penman, who ascended the Restigouche four years later, gives quite a different picture. He describes how, at the mouth of the Patapedia, which the Indians pronounce *Pat-a-pa-jaw*,[H] his companions took two big salmon during the evening fishing, "and the deep, black pool…seemed fairly alive with the hungriest of old veterans." When dark came, *Penman*, instead of going to sleep—as did his friend—went out with his two Indians who had decided to spear salmon by the light of pitch-pine flambeaux.

He recounts that "above the Patapedia, the Restigouche river fairly swarmed with fish and did not belie the reputation it had hitherto maintained… In the long reaches of deep, still water huge salmon lay motionless upon the bottom, and sculled leisurely away when disturbed by the passing canoes." There were "darksome pools and swift rapids and ever and anon sparkling rivulets of ice-cold water came leaping into its limpid bosom from the mountain-sides. And just on the verge of the bubbling foam a cast of the fly was certain to raise a splendid trout." He speaks of "a perpendicular cliff of naked granite (that) descended into a pool as black and inky as the realms of Cerberus. The Indians said there was no bottom there—at least it had been sounded by two canoe loads of cedar bark (the inner bark of the cedar made into a long rope—G.F.C.) without success—and their statement was confirmed, as far as it could be, by sounding with several hundred yards of fish-line. And yet," he goes on, "not six yards off, the bottom of the opposite side of the river sloped gradually, and the water was not more than three feet deep until it suddenly struck the inky line. It was frightful," he says, "to gaze aloft at the threatening cliff, and then contemplate the unknown depth of the pool below."

I know the spot, and it is as awe-inspiring as *Penman* describes it.

* * *

He speaks of the *Quah-tah-tam-Kedgewick* as being on the old maps; says this "name has since given place to the more humble one of *We-Tom-*

[H] I have heard white guides call it—*Pat-a-ma-jaw.*

Kedgewick, and the lumbermen had still farther contracted it to Tom Kedgewick." Today it is simply called Kedgwick.

"Two miles below this stream they (he speaks of himself and the Captain in the third person) passed a crumbling house which once belonged to a misanthropic Scotsman named Cheyne. Here, sixty miles from all traces of civilization, he sought a complete seclusion. When another man (attracted by the inimitable salmon fishing) settled down beside him he bought him out and thus purchased the solitude he valued, although he never made use of his additional acquired possessions. Three years ago his horse came home one day, saddled and riderless, and was so found by some passing hunter; but old Cheyne has never since been seen, and it is supposed that he was drowned in the river in consequence of the failure of an attempted experiment. He started for home" (doubtless from Campbellton) "with two full whiskey jugs at his waist-band, and, while *en route* tried to make an empty jug balance a full one."

"Since then," adds *Penman*, "another character, named La Farge, has established himself just at the confluence of the Restigouche and Tom Kedgewick, occupying the summer in hunting and trapping. La Farge has a wife and infant. *Penman* asked Mrs. La Farge if she enjoyed much society in those parts, to which she answered that she 'got along tolerable, but she didn't see much of her neighbours.' There was not a woman within forty miles!"

Where Mr. and Mrs. La Farge took up their solitary abode soon after Cheyne's death, there is now quite a village. Below this—a half mile—is the home and outfitting establishment of Mr. John Broderick (one of the finest and most obliging men I've met on the Restigouche); and beyond this again the Lodge of Mr. E. P. Rogers, Sr., of New York, who leases the water from the mouth of the Kedgwick to the Soldier's Pool—down the river.

* * *

Penman tells that the Captain had previously planned to go up the Kedgwick, while he had decided to canoe with his Indians up the Little Main Restigouche, and then, by the Waagan and Waagansis (the *sis* being the Maliseet diminutive for little) and the Green River, to the Saint John. So here they parted company.

On the Waagan Portage *Penman* was "surprised to find a spot where the trunks of the trees were covered with names and initials cut into them with knives—some bearing ancient dates and nearly overgrown with newly-formed bark. Larry (one of his Micmac guides) told him that these were the initials of all those who had crossed the portage, and it was the custom for every one to make his mark. Then, stepping aside, he pointed to a square post standing at the head of a scarcely-perceptible mound, and said, 'Here, man, get somebody makum mark for him.' *Penman* looked as directed, and read with some emotion this inscription:

Harry Baker
Died 1843. Aged 43 years.

"The lettering was neatly carved upon the wood. Larry told the history of that grave. A party of lumbermen had come thus far through the forest on their way to the portage. One of their number was sick nigh unto death. They had cared for him many days, and toiled faithfully to carry him out to the settlement; but it was useless to attempt the passage of the Waagan with such a charge, so they quietly strangled him and left him here to pass the river of death alone. They justified their conduct, to themselves if not to the world, by asserting that the man would have died anyway, and that it was better both for him and them."

For those of my brother-anglers who would like to read the whole of *Penman's* most interesting article, I would advise them to consult their Public Library where doubtless they will find Vol. XXXVI, No. 214, of *Harper's New Monthly* magazine.

* * *

I first fished the Kedgwick in 1925. At that period the late Mr. E. R. Teed, of Woodstock; Senator Gould, of Presque Isle, Maine; and Mr. G. L. White, of Grand Falls, were lessees of some nine miles of the river beginning at Two Mile Pool; and Mr. Teed had kindly offered me the privilege of fishing the water for a week beginning first of July—one of the very best weeks of the season. Not only are the fish large at this time of year, but they are fresh run from the Bay Chaleur.

I was met at Broderick's by Bill Ferguson who was to be my guide and cook. Bill, a stocky man about my own age, was as swarthy as an Indian with brown eyes that laughed when he was amused, and a wave in his black hair that would have won the envy of the present-day fair sex who spend a half-day each week having a hair-do. He had been born a few miles above Campbellton, and was familiar with every pool on the Restigouche and the Kedgwick. His four brothers also guided.

He introduced himself, shook my hand, gave me the "onceover"—which he later confessed was for the purpose of confirming or rejecting the account Mr. Teed had given him of me—and then, with a broad smile, stored my dunnage in his canoe, and told me where to sit. In a few minutes we were breasting the rough, swift waters of the Kedgwick. It was uphill all the way, but the river lacked the multitudinous boulders so characteristic of the Main Southwest Miramichi.

Just above the mouth of Kedgwick I saw an angler land a salmon. It looked to me like a twenty-pounder. I said to Bill, "That's a big one." He gave a low chuckle and remarked that *it* was a mere baby.

Bill made light of the work, and in fancy I can still hear the thud of his iron-shod setting pole on the rocky bottom, as constant "as the second-hand of a watch marks the passing hour." On the way we paused and fished Upper Two Mile, but if salmon were there they refused my fly.

Shortly before dark we reached the camp, set on a small plateau approached from the beach by a long flight of wooden steps. On the right was a gorge down which a brook—appropriately named White Water—tumbled to the river.

After a hearty supper we sat and talked for a while. Bill told me about his wife and family living at Flatlands. One boy was thirteen years of age and in another two years would be guiding. But he had for long been familiar with a canoe and had landed several salmon... Yes, there was a big run of fish in Kedgwick, and we should have good sport… (At the moment I never imagined how good!) He loved the river and the woods, and told me that once he had found in the woods a great hole the diameter of a flour barrel, into which he had thrust a twenty feet long pole without finding bottom. He thought it might have been made by the fall of a meteor. *Penman* tells of a like marvel, described to him by his Indian guides, two miles from Two Brooks. It very probably was the same hole described by Bill Ferguson.

* * *

I had a sound sleep that night, and awoke about seven o'clock to smell bacon cooking… After breakfast, and the dishes washed, we dropped down to lower Two Mile—a long, wide pool flanked on the right by a ledge of slate-rock where the water was quite rough. On the left shore was a shelving beach—a splendid place for landing a fish. As Bill dropped his lead anchor and hitched the rope to the cleat on the inner side of the gunwale, he said: "Now you can look for action."

We had it. I had not made half a dozen casts before my reel—a four-inch Malloch—roared like a lawn-mower; and the largest salmon I had ever hooked had my No. 2O Nighthawk fixed in its jaw. Never have I seen salmon behave so wild as those I hooked in this pool. This first one—in particular—turned somersaults, like an acrobat doing a continuous series of handsprings, for seventy-five yards or more, churning the water into foam as it went. But it did not leave the pool. It would spin off a hundred yards of line in a matter of seconds, then sweep to the left hand shore, or to the right, and race back towards the canoe, while I reeled in as fast as my hand could turn the handle. Then it would turn with such suddenness and make off downstream that my line hummed like the strings of a harp, and the rod bent in a bow. It felt as heavy as would a yearling calf. My arms ached and I wondered if I would ever land it. But I had a good rod—a twelve-foot steel-centre Hardy, and I gave it the butt whenever I thought necessary.

Finally Bill landed me on the beach, from which I played the fish; and after half an hour's fight I was able to work it into shallow water where he neatly gaffed it. It tipped the scales at a fraction over twenty-eight pounds. *(13)*

Naturally I was elated at my victory; and I wondered how many noble fish had been landed from this beach since anglers had first fished the Kedgwick. Perhaps, in 1867, *Penman's* companion (the Captain) had stood where I now was—playing his fish while his Micmac guides waited with that stoic and seeming indifference to time, space, and the excitement of the moment that is so characteristic of the race...

Bill put the fish in the canoe and covered it with grass and ferns; then we again went to the head of the pool, anchored, and I began casting. Almost as quickly as it takes to tell I hooked another fish. As with the first—and subsequent strikes—I saw no swirl; only there was a sudden tug, the bending of my rod tip, and the harsh music of the reel that set my nerves a-tingle.

After a battle royal we landed it—a twenty-five pounder. When it was killed and laid beside its mate, Bill said: "Now we'll go after another."

"Another!" I echoed. "Oh, no. I'm tired. I want to lie down on this beach and rest. Haven't we got enough for one morning?"

"They may not be taking tomorrow," protested Bill. "Better take 'em while they're in the mood... I have a feeling that tomorrow there'll be a change of weather. Not rain, but mighty hot. It'll make 'em lazy." (How right he was. We took one fish the following day.) "How about it?" he added.

"All right," I agreed reluctantly. "But if I go out in the canoe you've got to fish and, if you hook one, play and land it."

He gave me an odd look, as much as to say: what kind of an angler are you? "All right," he said; and I got into the canoe.

* * *

It has always seemed to me astonishing how *good* guides are able to pole upstream and then drop down to the precise spot where they had anchored a half-hour before, or, having seen a fish break water a considerable distance away, will anchor the canoe within casting distance. Many times I have asked, "Did the fish rise here?" and the answer was always yes.

Having anchored, Bill took the rod which I had passed back to him, and I settled myself comfortably in my seat to watch his efforts. He cast a beautiful line with perfect ease and precision. I confess I hoped he wouldn't hook a fish—at least for a good while. But my hopes were soon blasted. He had not made a dozen casts before the reel screeched in my ear and a big salmon went tearing down the pool.

"Here—", cried Bill. "Take the rod!"

"No," I said, "you've got to play it."

"All right," he said, "but take the rod 'till I get to shore. We'll play it from the beach."

So I took the rod, while Bill raised the anchor, and poled to shore and I had got out. The salmon had turned, run up stream to almost the precise spot where it had taken the fly, and I hurriedly reeled in the slack line until I *felt* the fish. Bill, had retreated up the beach a dozen feet behind me, so I backed up beside him and said: "Take the rod, Bill. You've got to play that fish. It was a bargain."

He grinned at me and said, "Oh, no. You play it. That's what you came to Kedgwick for."

"Look here, Bill," I replied, "if you don't take the rod I'll drop the tip and allow the salmon to run back to the sea." (Of course I was only joking.) "Besides," I added, "*I* want to gaff it."

As Bill reluctantly took the rod, he said, "Did you ever gaff a salmon?"

"No. But I can try," I answered.

"Well then," he advised, "if I can bring it in, clip it over the shoulder."

"I'm a Scot," I said. "I don't like to spoil a good fish. I'll clip it just ahead of the tail."

But it was half an hour's hard fight before I had the chance to fulfil my promise. Back and forth—up and down—the salmon explored almost every foot of the pool within a range of one hundred and fifty yards. It leaped six times, sank to the bottom once, sulked and was only roused to renewed activity by Bill tapping on the handle of the rod with the back of his hunting-knife. Finally, however, it showed its white belly and Bill, backing up the beach, gradually brought it into shallow water where I stood with the long-handled gaff. I made one swift stroke just ahead of the tail and transfixed it through the middle then, my eyes half blinded by the water it threw up, dragged it to shore where Bill was laughing his head off.

It was—as were the others—a female, and tipped the scales at twenty-four pounds. I took Bill's picture holding it, and later entered an enlargement in a photographic competition sponsored by *Rod and Gun Magazine*. It won a twenty-five dollar prize, was reproduced full page in the magazine, and bore the caption: "Dr. G. F. Clarke and his Micmac Indian guide holding a twenty-four pound salmon." Bill, as I have previously said, was quite swarthy.

We took three more salmon that morning: nineteen, twenty-three, and twenty-six pounds. Every fish hooked was landed. I attribute this success to the fact that they took the fly in heavy water, and that we were using a No. 2O. And I have noted—throughout the long years I have angled—that in strong water the fish are usually well hooked... They hook themselves.

* * *

At twelve-thirty o'clock we started back to camp. Like my friend Russell, on the Saint John, Bill was a lover of Robert W. Service's poems, and on this occasion, while the thud of his setting pole spelled out the minutes, he recited *Sam McGee*; and later, either while poling up the river, or coming back to camp from one of the upper pools, swinging his paddle, he gave me more of Service, although his rendering of them did not equal Russell in dramatic intensity.

I did not fish that afternoon, having had enough battles for one day. After a nap I sat on the verandah beside a smoke smudge to keep away mosquitoes, and watched the river flowing by.

* * *

I usually take a volume of essays with me, but find it almost impossible to read more than a little. Nor can I write anything save it might be a few notes. There are so many aspects of Nature to observe and reflect on. I am interested in the river; in the bird life: in the Kingfisher poised on the high limb of a tree that bends over the water; in its sudden plunge into the pellucid depths after a small fish; in the Osprey circling on tireless wings far overhead. I see the little Sandpiper, in its spotted-white waistcoat, running along the sandy beach and over the rocks. Every moment or so it pauses abruptly—as though it had forgotten something—then bobs and bows as if it were the disembodied spirit of some obsequious servant doomed forever to perform a penitential ritual. Finally, it flies a little distance up the shore, repeating its mournful "Peet!–Weet! Peet!–Weet!" and then again runs over the rocks, over the sand, searching, bobbing, bowing—

Farther down I see a doe deer—her hide, this season of the year, as red as that of a fox—emerge from the forest, pause and look to right and left, and across the river to see if an enemy—human or otherwise—is near, and, assured of her safety, step daintily over the cobbles to within a couple of yards of the water, where she again pauses to gaze on every side. I am fascinated by her deliberate movements. Now she turns her graceful head towards the forest. She gives her tail a few hurried flips and presently a young fawn—its red coat dotted with large white spots—appears and minces its way over the rocks to her side.

There is much to see; so much beauty to absorb and marvel at. Sir Thomas Browne, who was born in 1605—the year that De Monts and Champlain founded Port Royal—says: "There is something within us, but not for us, and it is the Spirit of God," and going on: "Whoso feels not the warm gale and gentle breath of this Spirit, though I feel his pulse, I cannot say he lives, for truly without this, to me there is no heat under the tropic, nor any light, though I dwell in the body of the sun."

"To a few," says Blake, "this earth is actually a heaven."

Yet many of us go from morning until dark day in and day out through all the years, and never *feel* the beauties that surround us on every side. A tree is only a tree; its mysterious birth and growth we never marvel at. A gorgeous sunset is only colour. A stream rippling over its rocky bed does not stir our souls; the moon, riding across the bowl of the sky; the snow blowing like smoke across the fields; the wild geese honking their way north in the spring, evoke no emotion. The flowers are but flowers. We are like Wordsworth's Peter Bell:

A primrose on the river's brim
A yellow primrose was to him
And it was nothing more.

* * *

Above the chatter of White Water Brook comes the faultless melody of the Veery—the little *Ta-né-li-ain* of the Micmac and Maliseet Indians. Not long ago it summered in the South. What marvellous instinct (or reasoning) told it that spring had come to the northland?—so that it spread its tiny wings and threaded the sky-lanes its ancestors had charted after the glaciers had retreated from the scourged earth, and sang their rapturous litany to the wandering tribesmen—long ages before the European white race had dreamed that America existed.

Are we—who have arrogated only to ourselves the ability to reason, and to possess a soul—which no one has been able to define: "losing that love for spring which among our ancestors rose almost to worship? That the perpetual miracle of the budding leaves and the returning song-birds awakes no longer in us the astonishment which it awoke yearly among the dwellers in the old world, when the sun was a god who was sick to death each winter, and returned in spring to life and health and glory; when the death of Adonis, at the autumnal equinox, was wept over by the Syrian women, and the death of Baldur, in the colder north, by all living things, even to the dripping trees, and the rocks furrowed by the autumn rains; when Freya, the goddess of youth and love, went forth over the earth each spring, while the flowers broke forth under her tread over the brown moors, and the birds welcomed her with song; when, according to Olaus Magnus,[36] the Goths and South Swedes had, on the return of spring, a mock battle between summer and winter, and welcomed the returning splendour of the sun with dancing and mutual feasting, rejoicing that a better season for fishing and hunting was approaching?"[37]

---

36 Author of *Historia de Gentibus Septentrionalibus* (*History of the Northern Peoples*), 1555.

37 Charles Kingsley, "A Charm of Birds". *Prose Idylls, New and Old*, 1873.

A Pagan custom. So are many the early Christians stole from our Pagan ancestors, and which we still celebrate in our church ritual. But I maintain that they were nearer to Nature than we are.

* * *

Hazlitt, in one of his famous essays says: "The English…are naturally brothers of the angle. This pursuit implies just that mixture of patience and pastime, of vacancy and thoughtfulness, of idleness and business, of pleasure and of pain, which is suited to the genius of an Englishman. He is eminently gifted to stand in the situation assigned by Dr. Johnson to the angler: 'at one end of a rod with a worm at the other.'"[38]

The foregoing might now equally be written about Canadians and Americans; for no people in the world are more angling conscious. But, of course, in salmon angling we do not use the worm any more than do Englishmen.

Personally I like to fish the fly just beneath the surface for half the thrill is to see the swirl the fish makes as it takes the fly. Then, of course, the wild music of the reel.

* * *

I would not care to live all of my summers in the woods. Even the excitement of my favourite sport would lose its attraction. A vacation is a few days snatched from time in which to take stock of our mental day book, and readjust the debits we have incurred during the rush and hurry of town or city. There is work to do in the world.

Thoreau, who carped at and criticized and condemned town and city life, did not remain more than a year in his board shack at Walden Pond. But I am glad he stayed that long; for although most of us who have lived in the country have been acquainted from childhood with those aspects of nature he chronicled with such meticulous fidelity, and "thought everything was a discovery of his own," he has left us a book that has wonderfully

---

38   From "Merry England," in *Lectures on the English Comic Writers*, 1819.

enriched our literature, and will never grow old. For he brought to his "discoveries" a freshness of mind that makes the old things to appear like new.

* * *

While we live we cannot divorce ourselves from the world, and when we die we become a part of the universal mother. I was once deep in the woods on an archaeological expedition and thought I was alone, but at midnight I was awakened by a radio turned on by some campers who had come and set up their tent near by. And I heard the voices of Toronto, New York, London, Paris, Rome, Moscow and the Middle East, announcing the news of the day.

* * *

The following year I again went to Kedgwick, and as before Bill met me at Broderick's. After I was seated in the canoe he referred to his photograph in *Rod and Gun Magazine* and said his wife was going to kill me for saying he was a Micmac Indian. I explained that the editor was alone responsible for assigning him as a member of that tribe. Then I added, "I suppose you're Scottish?"

"And Indian, and a little Chinese," he announced soberly, then laughed and said his wife had forgiven me after receiving the book *Chris in Canada*, I had sent him for Christmas. "You do know the woods," he added warmly.

Then in my middle-aged snobbery, I half apologized for writing a boys' book (I had published a novel the same year); I would now restrict myself to adult fiction.

"Oh," he exclaimed, "don't say that! If you only knew what pleasure *Chris* gave us, you'd continue to write books for young people." Then he told me how—during the long winter with his own and several of the neighbours' children congregated in the big kitchen about the stove—his wife had read aloud to them each evening a few chapters of *Chris*; and that twice more that winter she had read it through while they clustered about her. "So give us more, Doctor," pleaded Bill.

Later on, in its proper place, the reader will learn why I have particularly dwelt on my book for boys, and of Bill's reaction to it. For what happened twenty-six years later stands out as one of the most beautiful episodes in my life.

* * *

What does a salmon prefer? After fifty years I have decided that it is the fly you fish with, be it whatever pattern you use.

The thing is to keep your fly in the water. In other words, fish. On one occasion I used the same fly for three consecutive days, only taking it off to retie the leader when it became frayed. The fly was a Mar Lodge; but I am convinced that almost any other—of the right size—would have done as well. I hooked and landed five fish—all big.

My old friend, Albert Goodine (who has guided so many years) agrees with me: "If the fish is a taking one, and the fly is presented to it *just right*, it doesn't matter what the pattern is."

Yet I have seen anglers carry with them as many as two or three hundred flies of all sizes and patterns. A few flies suffice me. I prefer the Jock Scott, Silver Doctor, or Wilkinson (it doesn't matter which—for a salmon is not going to look them over and prefer the fly which has a few more tufts of a pheasant's tail than has the other). The Mar Lodge, Butcher, Nighthawk, Black Dose, and the Cow-Dung. This latter has yellow hackles, an orange woolly body, grey wings, and is so radically different from the usual flies that have been fired over the fish from the time it left the sea that it often does good execution. I need no others than those I have mentioned, save a few dry flies. Although a selection of smaller hooks is necessary, I do not like very small ones, nor extra fine leaders. I found three big salmon (during one week) lying dead on the shores of the Restigouche. My guide and I examined them and in each case found a No. 8 fly-hook fixed fast in the gills; the tiny eye of the hook had cut through the fine leader. A fish with a fly in its gills cannot live! These fish had been hooked in heavy water. At the same time, in the comparatively quiet pool below, while fishing with a double No. 4, and a double 2O, and a nine-foot twelve-pound-test leader, I took three or four big salmon.

One of the secrets of taking fish is to have the fly moving fast. This is best achieved by fishing with a thirty or forty foot line. Thus, by casting to the right or the left the current will swing it around on a line with the bow of the canoe at a much faster rate than it will a longer line. It is the usual practice of those making very long casts to keep bobbing the rod up and down (I have done it myself times without number); but, if you could see the fly in the water at the end of one of these long casts, you would find that all your bobbing has not made any appreciable difference with the movement of the fly. A fish will take if he intends to at all, either when the fly floats within range of its vision, or follow its curve and then seize it. But it *must* be moving at just the right rate of speed.

I had a very interesting and educative experience while with Bill Ferguson. He had drawn up his canoe on the lower end of a long gravelly bar for the purpose of putting a patch over a small slit in the canvas. While he was waiting for the sun to dry the canvas, I took my rod and fly box and began walking up the left side of the bar. Between it and the shore the river flowed in a series of ripps and glassy water. When about three hundred yards above Bill I came to a swift run that was as clear as crystal, and in about five feet of water saw eight big salmon, three side by side, the others bunched just below them. I had a Jock Scott tied to my leader, and after lengthening out what I considered the right amount of line by making a few false casts well below the fish, I dropped the fly just a few feet above the three leading fish. Almost as soon as it struck the water one of them left its position and followed it as the line made its curve and straightened out downstream. But it didn't take and a moment later it was back beside its mates. I tried again with the same result. Then I tied on a Wilkinson and cast out. Again the fish left its position and followed the fly until it had come to rest, but made no move to take it. To be brief, I tried several other flies, always with the same result. Finally, I again put on the Jock Scott, and shortening my line cast just above the nose of the fish. No sooner had it struck the water than the salmon took it with a rush and went tearing downstream. I yelled to Bill, who came with his gaff, and after a half-hour's play we had it safely on the beach. It weighed twenty-three pounds. The question is: did that salmon prefer the Jock Scott to the other flies? I do not think so. It is my belief that it took the fly because it had been *presented to it just right*, or that I had teased the fish into taking it, and that it would have taken one of the other flies just as readily. But, what is the lesson I learned from this experience—? Had I not *spotted* the fish I would have concluded, after a few casts, that there were no salmon in that particular place, and have gone farther up the bar or returned to Bill. Therefore I am convinced that often, in deeper or rougher water—where we cannot see the bottom—fish often follow the fly, and since we do not see them we make another drop. In other words, if we were more patient, and if the fly were presented properly, or moving at the right speed, we would more often have action.

* * *

At this period supplies for the Micmac Club, some fifteen miles above White Water Brook, were transported up the river by tow-boat—a long, wide scow drawn by two horses.

It was the first of August, and I was again on Kedgwick; this time with three companions: Doctor Grant, Charles Clark and Perley Marston. One morning the tow-boat stopped at White Water and one of the boatmen handed Bill Ferguson a message that made it necessary for him to go down to Kedgwick. Since it had been our intention to fish some of the upper pools—especially Wyers—Bill suggested that we board this craft and tow our canoes behind us. He would join us later; in fact he assured us he would overtake us before we got to our destination.

I had never before been on a tow-boat, so it was a new experience for me as well as for my brother anglers—Charles Clark, and Marston. Not so with Doctor Grant. Once, as a lad of fifteen, he had walked all the way from Fredericton, along the beach, the forty miles to Southampton keeping pace with the horses, and tripping the tow-rope when it was fouled by bushes or rocks. When he reached home the soles of his boots were half detached from the uppers.

What particularly amazed me was the condition of the horses. They were as fat as butter. I commented on this, and was told that tow-horses not only liked the work but that although they might be thin at first, they soon grew fat.

At Fall Brook, a stream whose water is a beautiful turquoise and contains nice trout from eight to twelve inches, we stopped to boil the kettle and have lunch. And here—as good as his word—Bill overtook us.

Later in the afternoon we arrived at a small camp where we were to stay the night, and the Doctor went up to Wyers Pool with his guide, Guy Ferguson—Bill's brother.*(14)* The Pool—as clear as glass—was filled with big salmon; two or three hundred of them. They lazily moved to one side of the canoe as it passed but, although the Doctor fished with his usual patience, they refused to take until nightfall; and then only when he cast below them and stripped his line in by hand. In this manner he hooked and landed two fish, each weighing about thirty pounds. I later fished this pool and found that the water was so dead that the little current would not carry my fly around fast enough. I therefore tried the Doctor's method and one fish took—a twenty-six pounder. Just above *Wyers* the river makes a sharp bend, the water is swift and here, with only a few yards of line out, I saw a salmon swirl up from the bottom, open its big mouth and take my fly; then, when I had raised my rod tip and it felt the hook, it darted downriver to the wide pool below and gave us a merry fight before we landed it. It too tipped the scales at twenty-six pounds.

The next day we proceeded downriver fishing the pools as we went. About two miles from White Water Brook—at Upper Five Mile, if I remember correctly—Charlie Clark fished. At any rate it was a deep, long, gloomy pool I didn't like. Here, at its head, Charlie hooked a very big salmon and it tore off his line until most of the backing was gone. The line was about twenty-five feet opposite to where he stood. He could see it clearly where it disappeared in the black depths. Suddenly he cried out in a loud voice: "Gosh, there's a hell of a hole in that pool!" Just then a big salmon leaped out of the water a hundred yards downriver. He saw it and yelled, "Say, there's another one!"

His guide laughed. "That's *your* fish," he said.

"Oh, no," shouted Charlie, "my fish is in that bottomless hole over there!"

Guy shoved his canoe out, ran his setting pole down along the line which had fouled on the branch of a sunken tree, and Charlie reeled in the slack as fast as he could. Luckily the salmon had stopped its mad career downriver and had come upstream. After an hour's battle it was landed and weighed thirty-two pounds. The biggest we took during our stay.

* * *

In the spring of 1950 Bill Ferguson made the same long journey as had my friend, Russell Boyer. But, if spirits return to the places they love best on earth, I'm sure that with each recurring June Bill's kindly shade will wander along the banks of the Restigouche and the Kedgwick, where although it will miss many familiar faces he once knew, there will be others of the brotherhood of the angle. And this recalls some lines of a poem which, although written about another salmon river, applies equally to the Restigouche and Kedgwick:

> New faces come. And old ones go—
> Each to his last-long hunting ground,
> But ever do thy waters flow,
> And peace and beauty gird thee round.
>
> Here sings at eve the hermit thrush,
> And, swooping from the sky's blue dome,
> The nighthawk breaks the tranced hush
> As the canoes come speeding home.
>
> What luck? Ah, luck enough to know
> The comradeship of guides and friends,
> The sky aflush with afterglow,
> The tranquil peace the river lends.[39]

---

39 An otherwise unpublished poem by GFC.

Six Salmon Rivers and Another

* * *

Those three years on the Kedgwick were among the happiest of my life. The year following the excursion with the friends I have before noted, the stretch of river again came up for auction. It was bid in by the Du Ponts of Philadelphia for $12,000 per year, and I transferred my angling activities to the Main Restigouche, the Tobique and the Miramichi. At this writing Kedgwick is leased by Frasers, and K. C. Irving, the latter paying $32,000 per year.

— CHAPTER VII —

THE RESTIGOUCHE CONTINUED

For many years the four miles of water below *The Soldier's Run*, on the Main Restigouche, was under lease, but about the year 1918 Harry Chestnut[40] suggested to the then Minister of Lands and Mines that there were many Province anglers who were denied the privilege of fishing the Restigouche, and that by exempting this stretch of water from lease and charging a rod licence, the fees collected would equal and very probably exceed the sum paid by the present lessees.

The Minister saw the wisdom of Mr. Chestnut's suggestion and, since the term of the lessee was terminating in a few months, it was forthwith called the Government Open Water. The first year or two, with Jack Russell in charge of it, the anglers who fished the water lived in tents on a wooded flat at the lower end of the western shore of Pool No. 3. Then Russell built a wooden camp on a high knoll on the opposite side of the river, into which water was conveyed from a nearby spring brook. At that time, and for several years later there was accommodation for six rods. Then, in the year 1945, two more pools were added to the Government Open Water and there was room for two more rods.

---

[40] Founder of the Chestnut Canoe Company, famous for its wood and canvas canoes.

Six Salmon Rivers and Another

One of the pleasing features was, and still is, a huge stone fireplace which doesn't smoke and takes a four-foot log.

When I first had the privilege of fishing this Government Water, the Ogilvy brothers—David, and John (who with their other brother, Hendry, held the riparian rights of four miles of water on the Tobique and operated Gulquac Lodge) had acquired from the Government Russell's concession and purchased from him the set of camps he had built. The brother, Hendry, still continued to operate The Lodge at Gulquac, and took both angling and hunting parties until about the year 1945 when the brothers sold their interests on the Tobique to the Frasers—the big lumber operators. Then Hendry joined David and John (popularly called "Jock") on the Restigouche.

* * *

For thirty years—without a break—I fished this water, and for the most part was accompanied by my friends, Doctor N. P. Grant, Charles Clark, and W. L. Kennedy. *(9d, 15a-b)* We usually stayed one week. The angling was excellent. In those first early years nothing but a narrow trail led from the highway (four miles distant) through the woods to The Lodge. It was therefore necessary for us to motor to Broderick's below the mouth of Kedgwick where canoes—sent by Mr. Ogilvy to meet us—conveyed us the five miles to our destination. These journeys downriver were most enjoyable save on one occasion when a thunderstorm overtook us. When our fishing was over for the week, we were poled back to Broderick's by our guides, and, although we had more leisure to enjoy the scenery, I always felt sorry for the guides who had to pole the canoes against the heavy current—especially after a heavy rain had raised the river a couple of feet.

On one of these trips up the river Allie Murray poled Charlie Clark. Allie is a superb specimen of manhood, six foot two inches tall, broad chested, straight-limbed, who at that time weighed 198 pounds. Charlie was 225 pounds; the canoe, besides his dunnage, contained two hundred pounds of salmon. At Soldier's Run the river makes a sharp bend and abruptly drops a foot over a rocky bar. This evening the water was white with foam and rushing with tremendous force. But, heavily laden as was his canoe, Allie

The Restigouche Continued

Murray—although he had lost the iron point off his setting pole—drove it with irresistible strength and skill through the tumbling waters, nor stopped for even a brief rest until he had reached Broderick's.

* * *

I think it was the year 1919 that fire destroyed a large portion of the wooded area of northern New Brunswick. But on the high ridges and hills bordering the Restigouche River several lordly pines escaped the conflagration, and today stand up tall, straight, and mighty of girth against the skyline—reminders of what the forest was like even before the white man came to the shores of Acadia. But between the cracks and crannies of the slabs of slate and rubble that spread from base to summit of the ridges and almost perpendicular hills, a growth of poplar and other trees has taken root. And Mother Nature, who knows no rest, has even grown flowers and ferns, and luscious blueberries for the wandering bears, and for man—when he chooses to climb for them.

* * *

The question of fishing on the Sabbath is not left to the conscience of the angler on the Restigouche waters. Not, I imagine, because the members of the Riparian Association are more pious than their less wealthy brothers on the Saint John or the Miramichi, but because they have decided that the fish should have a day off on which to forget the innumerable flies cast over them the other six of the week. And it is notable that, after a day's rest, one has a better chance of good fishing on Monday. At the same time the conservationist kills as many fish as he legally can.

One late summer, when most of the big run had passed upriver from the lower pools, one of the most famous of American magnates—having fished his own water and shipped several boxes of salmon to his New York friends—arrived with his wife at the Government Water—many miles above his own stamping ground. It was then in charge of Mr. David Ogilvy (already mentioned), a Scot who would not have allowed the King of England to take more than his allotted number of fish per week. *(15a)*

On his arrival Plutus inquired of the manager if it was true that he would be permitted to take only twenty salmon during his stay.

The Scot told him he had heard correctly. "Twenty for you; the same number for your wife—if she fishes."

"That's ridiculous!" returned Plutus. His wife joined in the discussion, and insisted that they should be allowed to take as many fish as they wished.

The Scot was firm. "No more than twenty, each," he said.

Being a man to whom nothing was ever refused, whose word was law in his own extensive business, Plutus insisted that the Scot should ring up the Department of Lands and Mines and ask for a special concession in *his* case.

The Scot informed him it was not a matter for the New Brunswick Government to decide, rather for the Riparian Association, which had caused the law to be made. He could—if he wished—ring up the manager, who lived at Campbellton, but assured him that it would avail him nothing.

The disgruntled magnate and his wife returned to their cabin.

When the Scot later told me about it, I asked him if Mr. and Mrs. Plutus got their forty salmon during their stay.

"Noo, Doc-torr," was the reply. "The guides saw to *that*... They were most indignant! They knew that if the concession had been made every angler on the river, from head of Kedgwick to the mouth of the Restigouche, would have heard of it. Besides, as you know, every guide is a fish warden." A guide can anchor his canoe in a pool where you may never raise a fish, or only a stray one, and, if you do not know the water you will be none the wiser.

The Riparian Association—which is the special brain-child of the Restigouche Salmon Club—has done a good job in influencing the Department of Fisheries at Ottawa to pass laws prohibiting net fishing in Chaleur Bay between Saturday night and Monday morning; furthermore, all net fishing must cease after the fifteenth of August. Besides these regulations the Association employs wardens to patrol the river and prevent poaching. In no other way can the leased waters, as well as those open to the general public, be preserved as salmon rivers. If the fish do not arrive at the spawning grounds in sufficient numbers, the net fishermen will also suffer...

Although a few salmon reach the dam on the Penobscot River, in the State of Maine, it is not generally known that the Hudson, Connecticut, and Kennebec rivers were once famous for their salmon.

* * *

Some of my happiest days as an angler have been those when the Ogilvys were in charge of the Government Water on the Restigouche; not only because I usually had good fishing (although on one trip I fished a week and did not take one salmon) but also because I had fished their water on the Tobique, and they were my firm friends. Jock *(16)* often guided me. He was a reader of good books, and much of our talk—when we didn't have a fish on—was of books, or of world events on which (being a Scot) he had very decided opinions. His father and mother had emigrated to New Brunswick in the 1860s, and he as well as his brothers and sisters had been born here. But, brought up in a settlement composed mostly of Scots, they had acquired and retained the rolling r's so characteristic of the clans. When I told Jock that the Ogilvys had been among the staunchest supporters of that magnificent man, James Graham, Earl of Montrose, he was very pleased.

He had many stories to tell of his experiences as an angler, trapper, and hunter; and to listen to him was an education on wild life. But I believe his fondest love was angling for salmon. He had the patience of Job and was never tired of instructing the tyro in the art of casting. He would stay on the water until darkness made it impossible to see where the fly was alighting. He it was who guided Earl Alexander, when he fished the Restigouche; and Premier McNair's daughter, Marian, when she hooked and landed a thirty-eight pound salmon from the deep waters of No. 1 Pool. My wife and I were guests of her father on this occasion and I shall never forget the modest pride on her face as she came up the path from the river, with Jock carrying the big fish.

* * *

One morning, a cold tenth of June, with the water high among the alders, Jock and I fished the *Run*, or No. 1 Pool, from which we took two medium-size fish. Then we dropped down below a small brook on the right at the head of Cheyne Pool. At that time I thought it was *Chain*, but after reading *Penman's* article in which he refers to the misanthropic Cheyne having acquired land below his grant at the mouth of Kedgwick, I had no doubt that the Pool in question was named after him and perpetuates his name even though the story of his life and tragic end is now forgotten. (Since then I have found the name on a Government map supplied me by the Department of Lands and Mines.).

Jock had barely dropped his anchor at the head of Cheyne, when, having filled my pipe, I stood up in the canoe to straighten my cramped limbs. At the same time I struck a match with my left hand, held the flame over the tobacco, and—with about fifteen feet of line out—made a short cast with my right. As the fly swung around on a line with the canoe, a big salmon rose like a torpedo out of the dark depths about four or five feet to the right of my fly, described a beautiful curve and took it. The reel screeched for the fraction of a second, then stopped as the salmon sank back into the bottom of the pool.

"Did you set the hook?" cried Jock.

"It is set," I replied (it had hooked itself); and still holding the lighted match over the bowl of my pipe, puffed until the tobacco was going nicely. Then, tossing the match into the river, I sat down in my seat.

"We—ll," said Jock, "that's a most accommodating fish!" For my line was still taut and the rod tip bent almost double. But suddenly, as though it had awakened to the fact that there was something unusual in its mouth that was annoying and from which it must escape, the salmon started downriver in high gear, tore off a hundred yards of line, leaped five or six feet straight into the air, fell back with a splash as though a yearling heifer had been thrown into the water, then continued on its course down the pool with the speed of a train with a record to break and a free right-of-way. I heard Jock behind me exclaim, "Yon's a verra big fish!" His anchor was already up, and he was paddling with all his strength after the fleeing salmon. "He's making up for being so generous when you first hooked him," he added.

The Restigouche Continued

I was able to retrieve about one hundred feet of line, but at this moment the salmon changed its tactics. It swung to the right, rose to the surface in a skittering dash that left a wake like a steamboat, and ran upstream past us, taking out line so rapidly that it gave a harp-like hum and threw off a thin veil of water that shimmered in the sunlight. Beyond the ledge on the right and past the brook, the dynamic creature sped, then, in midstream, flung its whole length out of the water to fall back on its side with a splash as loud as that made by the tail of a startled beaver.

"That'll take some of the ginger-r out of him!" chortled Jock, as he swung the canoe towards the left hand shore. "He's a thirty-pounder." (All fish are spoken as of the masculine gender.) "Don't play him too hard, Doctor"—for I was holding my rod high up and applying a good deal of pressure. Barely had Jock spoken when the fish made an abrupt half-turn and came straight for the canoe. Jock seized his setting pole, drove it against the bottom, and with a quick shove sent the light craft almost into the alders. Now the fish paused in its mad rush, came to within six inches of the surface of the water, and curving its whole body struck my leader a smashing blow with its wide flukes that—for I had quickly taken my finger off the reel—caused the drum to revolve with such speed the gears sang like a power saw cutting through a pine knot.

Fifteen more minutes we each struggled for the mastery, but with Jock manoeuvring the canoe, I was able to keep its head against the current. Slowly but surely it was losing strength. Said Jock, "We'll have to take that fish from the canoe. And it's too fine a fish to spoil with the gaff. I'll use the net on him." Now he discarded his setting pole, and, picking up his paddle, carefully sent the canoe into the centre of the river a little below where the salmon, a half foot beneath the surface, was still headed upstream, but making only feeble efforts as I reeled in and kept my rod tip high.

Jock gently dropped the anchor, seized his long-handled wide-mouthed net and dipped it in the water. "Can you get up, turn around, and sit on the bow?" he asked. I could and did. I could hear my heart pounding against my ribs, as I very gently applied pressure on the salmon's mouth. It slid over to within five feet above where Jock stood, his shoulders bent, his brown hands clamped about the handle of the landing-net. "Now," he said, "let him drop back. Easy—not too much pressure." I did his bidding. I saw the great fish over the net, then Jock lifted the mass of silver from the water, deposited it in front of him in the middle of the canoe and, as the salmon curved its body in the effort to leap, dropped to his knees on top of it. Even yet—so great was its strength—it lifted him a few inches, and I feared it would upset the canoe.

Jock reached for the piece of lead pipe that served him as "priest" and—although the salmon was still full of fight—managed to strike it several blows over its head which quieted it for all time. Then, wiping the sweat from his brow with the back of his hand, Jock said, "What a bonny fish! He'll go more than thirty."

It did. Thirty-three pounds on David's scales. But several days later (when I arrived home) I weighed the fish on the hospital scales and it still weighed thirty-three pounds. Doubtless when first landed in the canoe it would have gone thirty-four pounds at least… Anglers are as particular about ascertaining the correct weight of their prize fish as they are about receiving the correct change when they have made a purchase in a store.

Jock washed his hands, then filled his blackened pipe (I never saw him with any other) and I mine, and we sat a little while smoking and talking. Then he pulled up his anchor, fastened the rope, dipped his paddle—and we started back to The Lodge.

As I went I thought—for the hundredth time—of the gentle Walton; and there came to my mind what Venator said to Piscator, while they were resting in a bower of woodbines, sweet briar, and jessamine, and were soon about to part company. "And, my good Master," says Venator, "I will not forget the doctrine which you told me Socrates taught his scholars, that they should not think to be honoured so much for being philosophers, as to honour philosophy by their virtuous lives. You advised me to the like concerning angling, and I will endeavour to do so, and to live like those many worthy men, of which you made mention in the former part of your discourse… So when I would beget content, and increase confidence in the power, and wisdom, and providence of Almighty God, I will walk the meadows by some gliding stream, and there contemplate the lilies that take no care, and those very many other various little living creatures, that are not only created but fed, man knows not how, by the Goodness of the God of Nature, and therefore trust in Him. This is my purpose; and so, let everything that hath breath praise the Lord; and let the blessing of St. Peter's Master be with mine."

Piscator: "And upon all that are lovers of virtue, and dare trust in His Providence, and be quiet, and go a-angling."

And remembering that Walton is said never to have caught a salmon, I wished that he could have been with us this morning, and hooked and played my big fish that Jock dipped out of the fast-flowing river.

Now we were passing the tall balm-of-Gileads whose sweet, resinous odours filled the air; we rounded the bend and saw The Lodge, and the wooden float below it, and all the canoes of the other guides drawn up; and the Doctor, and Bill, and Charlie, standing on the bank waiting to learn what luck we had had.

* * *

As a rule, anglers familiar with the Government Open Water on the Restigouche prefer the *Run*, or, as it is often called, No. 1. This pool—as well as Cheyne, just below—was once part of the riparian rights of the misanthropic Scot whose tragic end, in the year 1864, has been described so graphically by *Penman*.

But who can account for the strange clinking—or bell-like sound on the right hand shore of the *Run*, a few rods below a high ridge of slate-rock that ascends as straight as a plumbline from the deep, black depths at the upper end of the pool?

It was Adelard Gallant—my French Canadian guide *(15b)*—who first drew my attention to the sound. The sun was shining brightly, the time about eleven-thirty a.m., the day very warm. We were resting a big salmon that had made a slow rise for my fly without taking. Said Adelard: "Do you hear that noise over there—among the trees?"

I told him I had heard nothing unusual; and he said: "Sounds like a little bell... Listen. Now—"

So I listened, and presently, barely audible, but wholly distinct, the *clink! clink!* fell on my ears; just two or three self-same notes, then ceased. In the almost deathlike stillness they seemed as uncanny as if they had come out of the blue sky.

I have heard them a score of times since, always at the same hour, and on each occasion the sun shining.

Adelard could give no explanation of the phenomenon, nor did he attribute it to any supernatural agency. I didn't tell him, nor any of the other guides, how old man Cheyne started on his forty-five mile journey up the river with two jugs of rum—one on either side of his saddle—and of how the horse arrived riderless at the lonely cabin at mouth of Kedgwick with one jug quite empty. But the following winter I told the story of old Cheyne to a friend of mine; and later on, in the evening (in speaking of the splendid fishing in the *Run*) about the curious clink! clink!—like a little bell—I had heard at that place.

"Ah!" he exclaimed. "Dinna you see the connections?"

I shook my head. He shot me an incredulous look, then said: "Of course old Cheyne had a bell on his horse's neck... Sure, and it's that what you heard... Or, if not that, it was the sound of the empty rum jug swinging against a buckle on the stirrup strap. And old Cheyne's bones—? Well, nae doot they're at the bottom of the deep, dark pool you told me aboot... And his soul—? Perhaps the good God, in His wisdom, gave it the same kind of lonely place he craved on airth... Will you have a pipe of my baccy?"

* * *

I had a most interesting experience one day with a sulky salmon. Steve Campbell, who was guiding me, saw the fish lying beside a small boulder to the right of midstream opposite an old lumber landing. We were on our way to fish the head of the pool some distance above and, as it was yet early in the afternoon, Steve said: "How about trying for that fish?"

I readily assented. Steve poled upstream a few canoe lengths, then turned, dropped back and anchored. I could see the fish quite plainly about twenty-five feet out and a little below where I was seated. After a few minutes I began casting. The fish made no movement to take the fly, although as I continued casting it occasionally opened its mouth two or three times in succession and waggled its tail. Finally, I passed the rod to Steve, who had moved up back of me, and he had a try. Once it half swung up from the bottom, but immediately sank back beside its rock. As the minutes passed we became the more determined to hook the fish—a twenty-pounder, we thought.

Finally, after an hour and a half, with myself casting, the fly floated down past the salmon a good six feet, and suddenly it left the bottom in one mad rush. My reel screeched and the line ran out. "Gosh!" cried Steve, a moment later, "that's not *our* salmon… He's still beside his rock!" After playing what was on the end of my line we landed a four-pound sea trout.

The fact is that the trout was closer to the fly than the salmon, and, although the latter meant business, the trout got it first. At any rate (whether it was thoroughly disgusted, or because of the commotion caused in netting the trout) his salmonship left his rock, and swam slowly upstream a hundred feet to some other sunken boulders.

We then proceeded to the head of No. 4 Pool, fished it without success, and about dark began paddling back to The Lodge.

Just as we were approaching the old landing, on the right of the rock where he had first seen the salmon we had tried so patiently to get, Steve dropped his anchor, and said: "Do you want to try for that fish?" I said, "No, Steve, I'm tired. He won't be there anyway. He left (if you remember) and went upstream."

"He'll be there," said Steve. "He liked that rock."

"All right, you try, Steve," and I handed him my rod.

Steve pulled off enough line to reach the rock, made a few shots downstream, then cast where he had assured me the salmon would be. There was a big swirl, a flash of silver, the screech of the reel—all in the fraction of a second—then Steve set the hook so quickly and hard the leader broke close to the fly and the salmon went off with a Black Dose in its mouth.

Steve was disgusted. I laughed, then apologized and assured him that probably I'd have done the same as he had. Then we went back to The Lodge; but I'm sure that Steve (one of the best guides and anglers I've known) remembered the occasion as long as he lived.

* * *

Too many people are busy piling up wealth they cannot possibly use and gaining power and position. They are like Christopher Marlowe's *Tamburlaine the Great*, only concerned with their own selfish interests. They are not really happy; for no matter how much they have of this world's goods, they worry lest some universal financial crash will rob them of their gains. About the year 1937 a friend of mine (living in a city that shall be nameless) asked me if he could invite one of the head executives of the firm for which he worked to spend a month at my camp during the hunting season. I said yes. I met him at the railway station on the day he arrived at Woodstock, and later drove him to the camp. He was a big man, physically; overweight; one whose nerves were shot. On the way down he told me that his doctor had prescribed complete rest. He assured me he had decided to wholly divorce himself from the home office and didn't want a newspaper of any sort...

Within two days he had set up a small wooden box on a tree at the head of the trail leading to the camp, and had made arrangements with the driver of a tote-wagon (carrying supplies to a lumber shanty farther on) to take letters to the post office at Millville, and bring back any mail addressed to him. A few days later he was sending telegrams to his firm, and to his broker, and receiving answers; also the *Wall Street Journal* and *The Times*. The result was that he made himself miserable, as well as his camp-fellows.

I was reminded of a man Izaak Walton tells about who had several well appointed houses, and was forever moving from one to the other. Being asked by a friend why he did so, he replied, "It was to find content in some one of them." But his friend, knowing his temper, told him that "if he would find content in any of his houses, he must leave himself behind him, for content will never dwell but in a meek and quiet soul."

* * *

One year, in mid-July, I had arrived at the Restigouche after a very heavy rain had raised the river a couple of feet, and turned it such a muddy-brown that one couldn't see the bottom a foot from the shore. However, it was now dropping; but I had never fished in such opaque water and doubted the wisdom of going out to try. My guide, Albert Goodine, said: "Harry Chestnut always liked it like this." That was enough for me.

We dropped down to No. 5, anchored, and I began casting. Suddenly, directly below us about forty feet, I saw something that looked like a piece of pulpwood bob a moment or two on the surface of the water; then another to the left. I said to Albert: "Are those objects fish?" He said, yes, that in such water they left the bottom for the slightly clearer water near the surface. So I lengthened my line and cast to the right of where I had seen them. Almost immediately I connected with a fish—about fifteen pounds. Soon after landing it I hooked another which we also landed. Twenty minutes later I was into a beauty that took us a half mile downriver. Finally we got below it, and Albert shoved the canoe against the alders. Now the fish took a run more than half-way across the river, then up past a big submerged boulder and stopped. "He's gone!" said Albert. I didn't think so, told him I could feel something heavy on my line. He thought it might be caught on the boulder, that the current against the "bag" made it feel like a fish. However, he pushed the canoe out, but soon found it difficult to get good pole-bottom. At the same time I was reeling in the slack line. Finally, when we were fifty feet below where my line was *caught on the rock*, my reel began to sing, and the salmon darted up and towards the opposite shore. Then—for it had had a rest—we had a merry fight for another half-hour; but at last I brought it in close to Albert, who had shoved his canoe in among the alders, which were all afloat, and he gaffed it. It was a strong twenty-seven pounds.

Harry Chestnut and Albert Goodine were right. Fish can see in muddy water. But, if the water is tea-coloured one might as well stay in the camp.

* * *

It was while the Ogilvys were in charge of the Government Water that I *first* appreciated the delight of eating smoked salmon. True, I had previously tasted the smoked product, but in every case it had been smoked until it was as hard as pemmican. David Ogilvy had learned the art (it is an art) by long practice, and his own particular preference was a three days' smoking rather than the usual period of a week. The result was, that far from the outer portion being as black as the hide of a New Brunswick bear, it was a beautiful golden colour. When you picked up a slab and held it at a slight angle, the flakes would separate and the imprisoned oil exude. One could, with fingers and thumb, readily pick up a gobbet of the delicious ambrosia and convey it to one's mouth. The fabled gods would have conferred on David the special accolade of their immortality. Of course this ritual (for it was a ritual with David) of three days' smoking was for his clients who did not want to keep the fish more than thirty days; for a longer keeping he submitted the fish to an extra two days in his smoke-house.

First the scales were scraped from the fish, and it was split down the back a little to one side of centre, the insides removed, then the spine with all its conjoined bones carefully dissected out. After being washed it was put in the salt barrel for twenty-four hours, taken out, washed and laid on a flat board to dry thoroughly in the sun, the while David stood by with a folded newspaper or a bush to keep off the flies. At the end of half an hour he placed the two halves of the salmon (or, if it was a very large one, cut it in quarters) on a wooden rack in the smoke house. On the floor he had a big iron kettle in which he put sticks and started a fire, to which, when well lighted, he added hardwood or firewood sawdust, which smothered the flames but did not put them out. The result was a slow and constant smoke. Occasionally—perhaps twice each day—he put in more sawdust, being careful that it did not break into flames and cook the fish.

* * *

Since then I have several times smoked some of my salmon after returning home. I made my smoke-house out of a big packing case of plywood, cut a hole in the top, and set over it an old oven that had originally belonged to a kerosene-burning stove. One side of the box had been removed; on this I put hinges, and had my door. I had a large iron pot similar to David's, and in this made my smoke. But instead of using all sawdust, I cut into suitable lengths a couple of sugar-maple saplings, of which we have many in the woods back of our house. I flatter myself that my smoked salmon was as good as that furnished by David to his sports. One autumn I also smoked two hams and the bacon sides of a one hundred and thirty pound porker, which my wife had first pickled for three weeks in a mixture of salt, molasses, and brown sugar. The result was that the hams and bacon smelled and tasted of wood smoke; and for a long time after it was all gone we could not abide the product that had been painted and injected with artificial smoke.

* * *

As a rule anglers prefer the June until mid-July fishing. Personally I am content with the last two weeks of July; and some of my very best fishing has been in August. I do not like heavy water when it is up among the alders; rather preferring it when it has dropped and contracted. Then it is more intimate as well as more beautiful as it winks and chortles its music over the bars; and since the shores are not flooded I can watch for the wild creatures that come out of the forest, and see the galaxy of flowers along the banks. Any tyro can hook salmon early in the season when the water is high and the fish fresh run. Of course, casting in low water requires more skill but then I enjoy taking a fish under such circumstances. On the other hand, I have seen salmon take a fly that fell upon the water with a splash and was encircled with a yard or two of casting line. One never knows when a salmon will take—or why. And this very fact is what gives zest to the sport of angling.

* * *

I do not go to a salmon river only to catch fish. As my friend, Doctor Grant, said more than once, getting the tackle collected, the trip to the river with friends, and, once there, sitting in a canoe, enjoying the scenery, listening to the birds' singing, and, above all, the knowledge that one is having a day off from the ordinary affairs of life make up half the fun of going fishing.

The year 1956, when most of the anglers had left the pools in the river below the Government Water, and no guests were booked for after the first of August, I enjoyed some of the best fishing I had ever had, taking thirteen salmon; four were slightly over twenty-two pounds, some less, and one a twenty-seven pounder that rose to my fly just as dusk was settling over the river. That same night I raised two other big fish, and during the week lost several. To sum up; I was only one less than the record taken for any week during the season.

* * *

I remember well one fourteenth of August—the last we were allowed to fish (the season has since been extended two weeks) my guide had dropped me down to the head of No. 5. Doctor Puddington, of Grand Falls, who came to The Lodge three days earlier, had recently undergone a surgical operation, and had with him his nurse, Miss Josephine La Plante, popularly known as "Jo". This morning he had decided not to fish, and arming her with his favourite rod, told his guide to take her down to Larry's—the pool that had been allotted him.

At breakfast the anglers present—including my friend, Bill Kennedy—had made up a pot of six dollars to go to the angler taking the largest fish.

Jo is a petite young woman with all the vivacity so characteristic of the French Acadians. Her guide set the canoe at the lower end of Larry's just below the mouth of a cold brook and within casting distance of a sunken rock—a favourite spot for big salmon.

I had already raised a good fish that didn't take, and was giving it the usual three minutes rest when I heard a heavy splash behind me, followed by her guide's voice, "You've got him!" In a few moments more the fish, with a hundred yards of line over its shoulder, sped past me, followed by the canoe. Jo had both hands clasped about the rod handle; her jaw was set, her eyes betrayed fear that the salmon would get away. Down the river they went. At times she was able to retrieve a few yards of line, only to have it taken back with interest. The salmon explored both sides of the river, then again started downstream. Never once had it showed itself; but from the way it acted both my guide and I thought it was either a very big fish, or a grilse that had been accidentally hooked in the tail.

Finally, a half-mile below us, the canoe was lost to view behind a point of land just above the ripps that led into the pool called *Pancost* (named after an angler who had taken a big salmon from it many years ago).

An hour passed and then, while I was fishing a little beyond where I had raised the salmon when I first dropped into the pool, we saw Jo's guide poling his canoe around the bend… Nearer and nearer they came. When they were opposite me I called out: "Did you land it, Jo?"

She nodded happily, then said, "But only *le Bon Dieu* and I know how my arm aches!" and she held up her arm and feebly shook it.

It was now one o'clock; time to stop fishing until the late afternoon, so my guide—Hendry Ogilvy—lifted his anchor and turned the nose of the canoe upstream.

Jo's guide had pushed his canoe ashore to get a drink of water from a little spring brook, so it was that I arrived back at The Lodge some minutes before they did.

* * *

We found Bill Kennedy, his guide, some of the other anglers, and David Ogilvy, standing beside a big salmon that lay on the grass. We were admiring it—a thirty-two pounder—when Jo and her guide appeared. In his left hand the guide held a four-pound grilse; his right was behind him well up his shoulder.

"Well," said Bill, "we're all in, so if that's the best you've got, I guess I've won the pot."

Then Jo's guide swung his right arm in front of him, his hand holding an enormous salmon he laid on the grass beside the other fish. It was not as long, but much greater in girth than Bill's fish, and as bright as a silver dollar, while Bill's was somewhat brown from having been in the fresh water several weeks. The scales were brought. Jo's salmon went a strong thirty-five pounds—the biggest fish taken on the Government Water that season. Bill was the first to congratulate her. We handed over the six dollars, and David Ogilvy further celebrated her victory by presenting her with a bottle of *ne-plus-ultra*. Needless to say, Jo soon opened it, and we drank to her health and good luck. She fully deserved her triumph, for she was a bonny fighter.

* * *

There is always keen rivalry between the guides. Each wants his "sport" to catch the largest number of fish, and the biggest one; and for his sport to be low rod is, he feels, an undeserved reflection on his ability as a guide. And when he staggers up the steep path to The Lodge lugging a couple of twenty-five pounders, or possibly bigger (although he tries to preserve a quiet dignity) his whole face shines; and when he drops them nonchalantly on the grass for the others—less lucky than he—to admire and guess their weight, you can almost hear him say, "Beat *that*, will you?" No prehistoric Indian ever exhibited to his tribesmen the scalp-locks at his belt with greater pride than that of the guide who beats his rival in the game of angling, even though his be a vicarious victory—for when he talks over his day's fishing with his comrades he invariably says, "I took so many fish today."

Even A. who guided me last year, and worked like a beaver in his efforts to make me high rod, will, should he be transferred next season to guide another angler, try just as hard to win the laurels for him—and for himself… He will love me, but I shall now be his rival in the noblest of sports.

For the most part these New Brunswick guides are splendid fellows. They are keen judges of human nature, will evaluate you after you have been in their company no more than a day; and I would rather have their approval and friendship than be accorded a knighthood.

* * *

Most anglers are gentle men, and friendly. As they pass you on the river it is with a wave of the hand, and: "Good luck! a tight line!" A few—faces fixed straight ahead—pass without even a nod. I wonder what they are thinking about. Once, a man past middle age, came alone to The Lodge. He was very wealthy. One morning there was some misunderstanding about the *pot* we had made up the day before to go to the angler catching the biggest fish. He maintained that *he* was right, and all the rest of us wrong, that on any subsequent occasion it must be put in writing. Then, after a glance around the table, he said: "When I was a young boy, my father told me *never to trust anyone!*"

None of us—and there were men present from his own country—made any comment. But, from that time forward, the *pot* was made up without asking any contribution from him. He was treated courteously; that was all. After the day's fishing he went to his solitary cabin, as he had previous to our brief altercation.

Sunday morning we left for home before he did. I saw him, standing in the doorway of his cabin—a pathetic-looking soul. I went to him, held out my hand, said goodbye, and wished him a safe journey. I shall never forget the look in his eyes—like that of a little boy who has been offered some object previously denied him—as much to say, do you really mean it? Then a smile flooded the wrinkled old face, and he said, "Oh!—thank you—The same to you." And then, a lump in my throat, I joined my companions. He was not to blame for his cynical outlook on life—it was the heritage his father had passed on to him.

* * *

I have previously mentioned Allie Murray (the guide who without an iron on his setting-pole, poled Charlie Clark up the freshet-flooded river to Broderick's). At that time he owned little more than the clothes on his back. I did not see him again until more than twenty-five years later… He has since told me that, when he was nineteen years of age, he walked thirty miles from Campbellton to the Upsalquitch River, to work on the log drive. He had purchased a pair of boots for nine dollars from the operator in charge of the drive. The drive lasted nine days. His wages totalled nine dollars. He walked back to Campbellton, and all he could show for his labour was his boots, the soles almost worn off!

At this writing he owns several apartment houses in Campbellton, employs a hundred men cutting lumber. In 1952 he took over the lodge formerly run by the Ogilvy brothers, and the control of the Government Open Water. He thoroughly modernized the lodge, installed electricity, built a kitchen that would win the approval of the most fastidious housewife, built four more cabins. In all these improvements he was assisted by his wife—a remarkably efficient woman. He purchased new canoes with outboard motors, and the guides no longer have to pole from the distant lower pools. He also owns one of the most up-to-date and attractive motels, with a trout-stocked lake in front of it, a short distance from Kedgwick, on the highway towards Campbellton. Not bad for a man who, as a mere lad, walked thirty miles to work on the log drive for one dollar a day!

* * *

About two years before Allie took over the Ogilvys, David had prevailed on the Department of Lands and Mines to widen the trail that led from the highway to the river, so that it was possible for anglers to motor into The Lodge door-yard. But it was anything but a good road, especially after a rain. Allie put on his own bulldozer, made the road wider, straightened it in places and gravelled it.

Not long after, the Riparian Association—composed of members of the Restigouche Salmon Club—made him their manager, and acts in an advisory capacity on various matters.

The Government Open Water ends twelve chains above the upper end of Little Cross Point Island. Below, to *Stillwater Pool*, are several fine fishing stands leased by the Restigouche Salmon Club. Then, two or three years ago, the club turned over this stretch of water to Allie, together with the beautiful lodge. Built several years ago it stands in a glorious setting just below *Down's Gulch Brook*. Below *Tracy Brook*, on the left, is the famous *Devil's Half Acre*, and opposite The Lodge is the *Trotting Ground*. The above stretch of water, with the Government Open Water, makes it now possible for Mr. Murray to take care of at least sixteen anglers during each week of the fishing season.

The Restigouche Continued

* * *

When *Penman* came up the Restigouche in the year 1867, such names as the *Devil's Elbow, Hell's Gate, The Devil's Half Acre*, the *Nigger Rafting Ground, No Man's Island, Grog Island, Brandy Brook*, and *Temperance Shoals*, had already been named. "Some incident," he says, "was connected with each name." He does not mention any lodges, only "occasionally a rude camp was discerned among the trees, and at intervals were mountain-slides a thousand feet high, down which the logs which have been cut come crashing with frightful velocity."

All this is now changed, for although the ridges and hills are still wooded, and present a wild aspect, there are lodges at intervals all along the river. And save for the Government Open Water the whole river, and some of its branches as far as the Quebec border, is under lease. To read some of the names of the members of the different clubs is like reading the American equivalent to *Burke's Peerage*. The magnificent pool, called the *Millionaire's Pool*, is descriptive. The New Brunswick Government—from the leases alone—reaps an annual harvest of almost eighty thousand dollars!

* * *

Some years ago, while fishing the *Run*, a salmon rose lazily about ten feet below my fly which had completed its curve, and was on a direct line with the bow of the canoe. I could see the great wake it made, its body wholly submerged. I immediately stripped off a strong yard of line and allowed the fly to float downstream. The salmon swirled and took it with a rush. This was a trick my Indian friend, Noel Moulton, told me. "Push it in its mout," he advised. (As in the thunder, he didn't pronounce the h.)

On another occasion, when a salmon rose and came lazily toward the fly, I began drawing in the line with my hand. The fish took. I saw Guy Ferguson do the same on the Kedgwick after a salmon had come twice without connecting with the fly. I remember well his, "Got you!" as the salmon, following the fly to within a few yards of the canoe, finally grabbed it.

Six Salmon Rivers and Another

The Run, Cheyne, No. 3, Larry's, No. 5, Pancost, Nos. 7 and *8*—I have fished them all scores of times; and, although Allie Murray now has more pools available, I prefer to fish the Government Water—not because it produces more, but because of old associations with loved companions, most of whom have now passed on—I shall not say to a better world, for this is beautiful enough. Golden streets and walls of jasper contain no allure unless there be plenty of trees and little rivers. No; the Almighty made for us, right here, a paradise. The trouble is that man, by his jealousies, and greed, and lack of understanding of the rights of his fellow creatures, creates all the discord and strife.

To return to a well-remembered river is like going back to the place of one's birth.

* * *

How many evenings—after fishing the upper pools—I have sat in the canoe and watched the dark shoreline slipping past; and then, exactly at nine o'clock, seen the Woodcock—a fluttering line against the lighter sky—as it sped from the left hand shore across the river and beyond the growth of poplars and white birches just above The Lodge. I can hear Albert Goodine's voice back of me as he plies his paddle: "There it goes! You could set your watch by it!"

Off in the distance, on the knoll, a light shines from the verandah—like a friendly hand welcoming us to an evening of conversation before the open fire; and then—sleep.

Year in and year out a Whippoorwill, called by the Indians *Hu-wip-o-lis* (which more nearly expresses its jocular command) perches in a tree near our cabin, and with tireless iteration insists that someone must be punished. Although not always as punctual as the Woodcock, it arrives sooner or later to render its verdict, which it keeps up for an hour or more, then—as though exhausted—takes a recess, to start in again before dawn; and finally, when we are all awake, steals away like a mischievous schoolboy.

And once, at midnight, I heard a White-throat Sparrow singing its brief notes—as clear as crystal. Had he awakened to serenade his mate, at this nocturnal hour? Perhaps—but I think he was rejoicing in the only way he knew how—and the best—that the starlit night was so beautiful.

* * *

I have taken many fine fish from *Pancost*—for many years the last pool on the Government Open Water. At the lower end, on the right, is a cone-shape, almost perpendicular hill eight or ten hundred feet high. It was burned over in the fire of 1920, but now is partially covered with a growth of poplar, birch, and other trees. Back of it is a level plateau where blueberries of extraordinary size flourish. On the river side one can plainly see what looks like a path caused by occasional avalanches of rubble and glacial sand. I had never thought it possible for any animal to use it.

Half-way down the pool, on the left, is Hilda's Rock (a flat boulder whose top is just a foot or so below the surface of the water). Here, years before I had fished the Restigouche, a lady known only to the present guides as "Hilda", hooked an enormous salmon which took the line over its shoulder and was not brought to gaff until it had reached the deep pool below Little Cross Point.

With Jock Ogilvy as guide I fished Pancost one day in mid-June, and at Hilda's Rock hooked a very big salmon that ran the width of the river at the first rush, then started down the ripps and we after it as fast as Jock could pole the canoe. There was no stopping it; it went like a train with a record to break and a free right of way until we were several hundred yards below Hilda's Rock. Then Jock got below it and landed me on a bit of rocky beach from which I played the fish. Once I had it almost within reach of the gaff, but it either saw Jock, or his shadow, and again rushed upriver. Then the backing to my casting line broke.

Said Jock: "I had a verra strong feeling that we were predestinated not to land that fish."

"Oh, well," I replied, "it was good fun while it lasted. Let's smoke a pipe."

* * *

One day Charlie Clark and his guide fished Pancost. For a while the morning was calm, then—as so often happens at Pancost—a wind came up and made casting difficult. So Charlie said: Let's land and have a drink of water from that nice spring on the right." Later, Charlie told me the following:

"We had barely got to shore, had a drink, and seated ourselves, when we heard a whistling, then a roaring sound, and around the bend above us came a waterspout. It was fully fifty feet high and as big in circumference as two molasses puncheons. For half a minute it whirled like a mad dancer right in the middle of the river where we'd been fishing. With every whirl it gathered up more water. Finally it lifted itself straight up into the air and disappeared over the tops of the trees on the opposite shore. If," added Charlie, "we had not come to shore when we did, it would have carried us with it—canoe and all."

"Are you sure," I said, "that it was only water you drank?" He gave one of his Rabelaisian gusts of laughter (laughter that Joe Sullivan, who came to The Lodge the following day, said was worth coming a thousand miles to hear) and said: "That isn't the whole of it, Doctor. That waterspout took all the wind away with it, so we dropped down to Hilda's Rock. I had made a few casts when, below us, on our left, we heard a crashing among the bushes, and the biggest bear I've ever seen rushed down the bank, jumped into the river, swam across to that big hill and tore up the path like something crazy; the rocks and gravel shovelling back of it with every leap it made. Finally that great bag of loose bones, flesh, and hair, reached the top and disappeared... Do you know, Doc, I think that waterspout just scared hell out of it. At any rate, I said to Burt: 'Let's get back to camp, or God knows what next we'll see.'

"Burt said: 'There should be a fish to the right of Hilda's Rock.'

"'Fish—?' I said. No, I wouldn't stay any longer if Hilda were here in all her glory!' So he upped with the kitty, and here we are." He ceased, and I said: "Did you say you had only one drink of that spring water?"

The gust of laughter that came from his great chest seemed to shake the rafters of The Lodge. (Oh, it was good to hear!) Then he sobered. "Do you know, Fred," he said, "you won't believe the truth when you hear it. Now if I had lied—" He gave another roar of laughter, and said: "Your parents should have named you Thomas—you know—that Bible chap—Thomas the doubter."

PHOTOGRAPHS

—— PART TWO ——

GFC holding a salmon, probably on the Miramichi, c. 1924

a. Russell Boyer and Angus Bernard at Russell's camp, c. 1944

b. Jane Bernard (GFC's elder daughter) preparing food at Russell's camp, c. 1944

Russell Boyer

GFC with 28-lb. salmon, Kedgwick River, 1925

Guy Ferguson gaffing a 23-lb. salmon on the Kedgwick River, c. 1925

a. Back row, from L: unknown young man, Dr Grant, Bill Kenedy, Charlie Clark, David Ogilvy, GFC. Front row: On left, probably a cook. The other three are probably guides. Probably 1937.

b. Seated: Bill Kennedy, GFC, Dr Grant. Standing: unknown, Adelard Gallant, unknown.

Anglers and Guides.

Jock Ogilvy on the Restigouche

"The Million-Dollar View"—the Narrows, Tobique River, before 1951

GFC with two days' catch, Gulquac Lodge, Tobique River, May 26th 1927

a. Noel Bear smoking meat, painting by Tappan Adney, c. 1893

b. Tom Moulton, probably 1890-1910

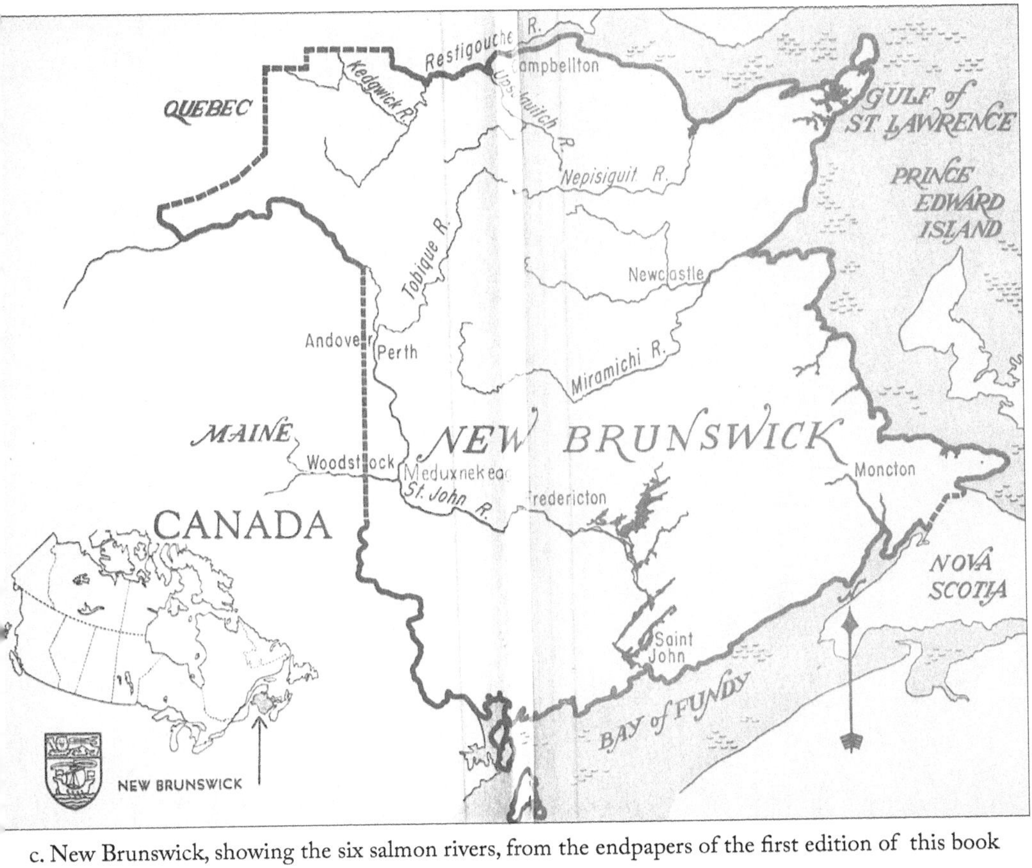

c. New Brunswick, showing the six salmon rivers, from the endpapers of the first edition of this book

— CHAPTER VIII —

THE TOBIQUE RIVER

The Tobique River was evidently called such after an old Indian named Tobit, who in the late seventeen-hundreds lived in a bark wigwam on the point of land where now stands the Indian village of Maliseet. Here the Tobique, or Nagoot—its aboriginal name—vents into the Saint John opposite Andover, and about a mile above the village of Perth.

Tom Moulton—a Maliseet Indian—was born on the Tobique Indian Reserve. *(19b)* As a young man he had spent part of his time at Moosehead Lake, in northern Maine, and the remainder at his old home. In both places he guided and trapped. Many times he had portaged his canoe over the famous Northeast Carry to the Saint John waters. He had run Big Black and Little Black rapids, and finally safely delivered his "sports" at Perth whence they had taken the train to their homes. He had guided on the Restigouche, Upsalquitch, the Main Tobique and its furthermost tributaries. He had poled the Left Hand Branch to Nictau Lake, portaged to Bathurst Lake and run the Nepisiguit. He had poled the Right Hand Branch to Trowsers Lake and paddled a dozen others. With old Noel Bear *(19a)* he had beat a snowshoe trail to the headwaters of the North Branch of the Main Northwest Miramichi, and hunted and trapped the vast wilderness through the very heart of the highlands and across the great central plateau to the head waters of the Little Southwest Miramichi.

Six Salmon Rivers and Another

* * *

After he married Eva, a Passamaquoddy Indian, he returned permanently to the Tobique and lived in a house on a high, level terrace just above the head of the Narrows below which, the McNair Government built a dam to develop electric power to serve New Brunswick industries.

Previous to this he and his kindred at the Point—two miles distant—angled for salmon at the head of the Narrows, at several pools below it, and in the Saint John itself as far as the Devil's Rocks. But when he grew older, his favourite pool (or run) was opposite Red Rock, three-quarters of a mile above his home. Sportsmen came and he guided them… One day, standing beside Tom's house gazing up the river that rippled over the bars and finally, constricted by the high palisades, rushed through the gorge spanned by the suspension bridge, one of his guests said: "That's a million dollar view, Tom!" And although he evaluated it in terms of money as so many of us do everything above and below ground, he was nonetheless sincere in his appreciation of its grandeur.*(17)*

* * *

Red Rock (where Tom's guests landed salmon, and he so often cleaned a fish, split it down the back, and then, fastening it to a slab of wood, broiled it in front of a little fire) is now under water, as is the site of Tom's house in which he and Eva lived so many years and enjoyed the "million dollar" view; as is the path leading to the spring at the base of the hill; and the spring itself; and his garden plot; and the little flat below the house where I had dug and found many of the stone artifacts his remote ancestors had chipped with such infinite patience.

Before the dam at the Narrows was quite completed Tom died. I followed the funeral procession over the steep highway to the height of land and down to the village of Maliseet, then to the Roman Catholic Church—dedicated to God and Saint Ann—in which he had been a devout worshipper… I stood in the little cemetery, while the Franciscan priest intoned the last rites, then came sadly home. He had been a good friend. He had been a part of Tobique. He *was* Tobique—

The Tobique River

* * *

As I have said earlier in this, the Ogilvy brothers owned the Riparian rights of three miles of river on the Tobique. These included several splendid pools from about a mile above Big Gulquac stream, to *The Priest's Rock* below Little Gulquac.

From the highway that leads from Perth to Nictau—a distance of fifty-four miles—a narrow but good road winds three miles through the woods to the Ogilvy water. In this secluded paradise, the brothers built a Lodge they named Gulquac, and several commodious log cabins (suitably appointed) to house their guests during the angling season. When September fifteenth came, hunters of moose, deer, and bear, arrived. They were conveyed over the eighteen-mile portage to Trowser's Lake, the centre of a famous game country.

* * *

I do not remember what year it was that I first fished the Ogilvy water, but think it was 1920. I went with Doctor Grant and Charlie Clark. Another year we took along Bill Kennedy—the Doctor's brother-in-law. *(9c)* Bill had never fished before, and the Doctor had loaned him a rod. He was stationed just below Little Gulquac, and I was fishing The Priest's Rock only a short distance below. Suddenly I hooked a good fish. It went tearing down the pool for a hundred yards then leaped clear of the water. Bill saw it and said to his guide: "Did you see that big salmon jump below where Doctor Clarke is fishing?" His guide told him it was my fish. Later, Bill told me he "was scared stiff." That if that was the way salmon acted, he didn't want to hook one.

However, after lunch we all moved farther downriver, and Bill hooked a fourteen-pounder. He was standing on the beach at the time, and during the play the reel dropped off his rod. Luckily the fish had decided to take a rest between the halves. Doctor Grant, being near Bill, restored the reel to its seat, and he reeled in the slack line. I was on the opposite shore watching the fray, and I can yet see Bill lifting one hand every few moments and wiping the sweat from his brow. We all shouted instructions. Now he would back up, the next moment he was running to the edge of the water. But finally he brought the fish in close enough for the guide to net. Then Bill incontinently flopped down on the beach and said, "My God! I never thought salmon fishing was anything like this!" He was spoiled.

The day after he returned home, he drove the sixty-five miles to Fredericton and purchased, from R.T. Mack, a Hardy rod, reel, line, and flies—a one hundred and fifty dollar outfit.

* * *

During the last depression, Bill—as hundreds of thousands like him—was hard hit. At one time he could have cashed in for half a million dollars. We were at Gulquac when the final crash came. I remembered we had just sat down to breakfast and had given our order when Hendry Ogilvy opened the door, and said: "Mr. Kennedy, you're wanted on the telephone." Bill rose to his feet, told us not to wait for him, and left the room.

After twenty minutes he returned, sank into his seat, and said: "Boys, I'm ruined!" Then he went on and told us that his banker—who held eighty thousand dollars of his stock as security—had phoned that he was selling it. Bill had pleaded with him to wait until he got home, but the banker was adamant.

We told Bill how sorry we were even though we realized that words were cold comfort, however well meant. Finally he said: "Now is the time to buy—if I had anything to buy with." A few moments later he looked out the window, where the river was sweeping past The Lodge, and said: "Well, boys, I'm going to land a twenty-pounder today." What splendid courage! Everything—the accumulation of years was gone; yet he could rise above the blow and think of fishing; of hooking a twenty pounder! He did. The fish weighed twenty-two pounds. I saw him land it.

The following year he collected together one thousand dollars, bought the low stock, sold it on a rise, reinvested it and did the same. Twenty years later he had made a small fortune and continued to fish the Restigouche until his death. I hope he has found little rivers in the other world.

The Tobique River

On May 26th, 1927, David Ogilvy telephoned us that there was a big early run of salmon in the Tobique, and asked us to come up. We agreed to go but, just a few hours before starting off the doctor was called to a home in the country to attend a woman who was in labour. He told me to go ahead, and he and Bill would join me in a couple of days.

Jock Ogilvy guided me. We first went to the pool opposite Big Gulquac where I landed four salmon. Finally I said: "Jock, there should be an old Indian campsite over there—" pointing to the right hand shore.

"Na doot," he said. Then I asked him if he would kindly put me on shore…

The following year he said to me, "Do you know, Doct-orr, I was awfully disgusted with you last year. There was the river filled with salmon just aching to be caught. And you said: 'Please put me to shore, Jock. There should be an old Indian campsite there.' So I pulled up the kitty, and landed you. Then you began grubbing among the roots, and turning over the thick moss disclosing arrowheads, knives, spearheads, and hundreds of flint chippings. In a few minutes I was on my knees beside you. And soon that place looked as though a hungry bear had been digging for ants. Funny thing was, that although I wanted you to hang up a record catch of salmon, I forgot all about the fishing myself!"

Later in the day I took two more salmon, and the following day two— one a twenty-pounder.*(18)* This last was in deep, glassy water. The canoe was anchored above and to the right of the fish, which came five times without taking the fly. Then Jock said. "We'll try a different position, Doctor." He handed me the paddle and asked me to turn, facing him, and paddle hard while he drew up the anchor. Then, with his setting pole, he placed the canoe on the opposite side of the fish within shorter casting distance than before. Immediately the fly had swung across the salmon's line of vision it took it with a bang… On other occasions I have cast directly over a fish and then quickly began to strip in the line by hand, with the result that the fish rose, followed the fly and took it.

That evening the doctor and Bill arrived. They asked me what luck I had had. I told them. "Well," said the Doctor, "I helped add to the population of Carleton County—I landed a nine-pound boy!"

Although most of this early run had passed, both the Doctor and Bill got a couple of salmon each. Then that night it poured with rain, raising the water two feet and turning it into a brown flood, and any other fish in the river refused to take. Had we been able to remain until it began to drop even a little, my friends would doubtless have taken more fish.

* * *

I have often heard it said that salmon will not take during a thunderstorm. This was disproved one day the Doctor and I were at Ogilvy's, on the Tobique. The Doctor went to the Gulquac Pool, and I above him to the Dead Pool. Hardly had we arrived when there came the dull sound of thunder; the sky became overcast with black clouds and in no time the rain poured down on us. During this torrent—which lasted an hour—I hooked three good salmon, and lost them all after a brief fight. Four times the canoe became so filled with water that we had to go to shore and empty it.

Finally the storm passed, and although I continued fishing I raised no more. Then we dropped down to the mouth of Gulquac and, seeing that the Doctor had left the pool, Hendry Ogilvy—who was guiding me—said: "We'll try here." (The doctor had fished the pool proper—on the opposite shore.) On the second drop I hooked one of the wildest fish of my life. It ran clear across to the opposite shore where the water was very heavy, jumped, rushed up the right side of Gulquac Island for fifty feet or more then downriver, back opposite me, sank to the bottom, gave its head a few shakes and my line went slack. "He's gone—!" groaned Hendry.

But it was great fun while it lasted.

When I got back to The Lodge, I learned that the Doctor had hooked ten salmon and landed three of them during the thunderstorm.

Although at that time I did not mind the lightning, I have since decided that to use a rod with a steel centre is tempting the fates, and I am quite contented either to go ashore and get under our upturned canoe, or else return to the camp.

When I have hooked and landed a salmon I usually pass the rod back to my guide and ask him to fish. Then I light my pipe (both dear old Izaak and his friend, Cotton, smoked, although many of the godly—including King Jamie—hurled anathemas at those who used the "lively image and pattern of hell")[41] and settling comfortably in my seat, enjoy the informing companionship of the river, and at the same time watch the casting of my guide. One can usually learn something from a good guide, and most of mine have been excellent anglers.

One day Jock told me that, while he was guiding a sport in the Gulquac Pool, a big salmon leaped right into the man's lap. He gave a yell, picked it up and threw it back into the river. "It was an example of refusing what Providence sent him," said Jock. As a matter of fact, one day when I was fishing the Restigouche, I hooked a grilse and it leaped into the canoe between me and the guide.

* * *

On a fishing trip I usually wear woollen underwear. Then, should I get wet, I am still warm. Not so with cotton. It is an abomination, as I learned this last August when my raincoat absorbed a prolonged shower. I always take along a heavy sweater, and a mackinaw coat. The very best raincoat is either an oilskin—such as deep-sea fishermen use—or one of those antique black rubber coats that can still be bought at some country general stores. All others I have tried—and they have been legion—do not shed rain—they absorb it! It is also advisable to take along two or three pairs of woollen socks, a pair of ankle-length rubber boots, and a sou-wester for the head. With these one can face the elements and return to camp dry.

---

41   Quoted in *The Compleat Angler*.

— CHAPTER IX —
THE UPSALQUITCH

Upsalquitch, or *Ap-set-kwetch*—its aboriginal name, which means "narrow going" in both the Micmac and Maliseet dialects—is aptly descriptive. Although the lower part for some twelve miles—is spread out, it soon narrows and enclosed by high ridges, in places almost mountains, with here and there deep gullies, or crevasses down which ice-cold brooks rush tumultuously to mingle with the crystal-clear waters of the river.

The Upsalquitch enters the Restigouche on its south side, twenty miles from Campbellton. Swift it is but easily canoeable. It twists and turns (with occasional long straight, stretches) between the hills. It is one of the most fascinating rivers I have ever seen. The land on either side is settled to the upper end of Ferguson's Turn. Above this were only three Lodges: that of Miss K. De B. Parsons; Myles Brown's, five miles above (a Government warden's camp above Crooked Rapids); and a set of now unoccupied camps at The Forks—the Junction of the Northwest and the Southeast Branches. All this is a vast wilderness that stretches to the Nepisiquit, the Tobique, the Miramichi waters, and beyond these more wilderness to where settlers in times past cleared their acres and established themselves.

In 1867, when *Penman* and the Captain went up the Restigouche, they stopped at the mouth of the Upsalquitch. *Penman* says they took several three-pound trout; and that Upsalquitch is famous for its excellent trout fishing. But whatever the Upsalquitch may have been in the year 1867, it is far from renowned today for its trout. Only occasionally can one catch enough to fill the frying-pan.

Five years before, in the early autumn of 1862, Captain Dashwood with two Indian guides, poled up the Upsalquitch, which he describes as containing few salmon and those of small size. Since he found such poor fishing on the Restigouche the following year, we must conclude that he was either a poor angler or else in too much of a hurry to reach good moose country (which was his primary object) to explore thoroughly the many fine pools on this very important river. But it is quite true that, save for a rare twenty-pounder, the average Upsalquitch salmon does not go over nine or ten pounds. At any rate, salmon angling is not at its best in early September. But he recounts that his "Indians speared some white fish which were excellent eating."

They journeyed seventy miles from the mouth of the Upsalquitch, then landed at the beginning of a portage on the Northwest Branch, left their canoes, and from thence for three days travelled through the woods—carrying their supplies on their backs—to Lake Nictau, at the head of the Little Tobique. Here they found an old birch-bark canoe, patched it, proceeded to the head of the lake then portaged for three miles and launched the canoe on the first of a chain of three lakes forming the headwaters of the Nipisiquit River. Reaching the river, they paddled down it for twenty-five miles, then discarded their canoe and travelled overland to the head of the Sevogle tributary of the Miramichi. Two months from the time he left the Upsalquitch he arrived at Newcastle, and in a short time had rejoined his regiment at Saint John. Since he, as well as many other members of the Imperial Regiment that garrisoned New Brunswick until 1867—when the last of such regiments were withdrawn from the Province—spent much of their time hunting and fishing, we must conclude that their military duties were not very exacting. But from the account Dashwood has left us of his quite remarkable journey through the wilderness of Northern New Brunswick; and from an earlier wilderness journey by Lord Edward Fitzgerald when in thirty-five days he walked on snowshoes to Quebec; as well as accounts of their travels left us by other Army officers, we have most interesting and valuable narratives dealing with hunting and fishing, with garrison life, and with the early settlements. But among these notable—and far transcending them all—was the famous William Cobbett[42] whose name is indelibly etched on the tablets of time; of whose multifarious writings Hazlitt says… "Might be said to have the clearness of Swift, the naturalness of Defoe, and the picturesque satirical description of Mandeville, if all comparisons were not impertinent. A really great and original writer is like nobody but himself."[43]

* * *

From the extreme limit of Miss Parsons' water, of which she had the riparian rights, the Upsalquitch is Government controlled. Formerly, it was leased from Boland Brook—above Miss Parsons'—to The Forks, and for some thirty miles both on the Southeast and the Northwest Branches, to a Mr. Pratt of New York. For thirty-five years Mr. Pratt, Senior, and then his son, John, controlled this vast stretch of water. But in 1952, the lease having expired, and the water again coming up for auction, the Government decided to withhold from lease the stretch of river from Popologan Brook to The Forks, as well as both branches; the whole to be known as Reserved Water, certain stretches of which could be fished by anglers paying a stated rod licence fee per day. This change of policy has been a great boon to those lovers of the angle—both residents of the Province, and those from the United States.

The intervening stretch—that is, from Boland Brook to Popologan Brook, or nine miles of water—was bid in by Mr. Myles Brown in 1952 for nine years at $4,000 per year, and he purchased the magnificent Lodge at Two Brooks from Mr. John Pratt.

---

42 Radical English journalist, 1763-1835. He lived in New Brunswick for six years as a young man.

43 Hazlitt, William, "Character of Cobbett", *Table Talk*, 1821-1822.

Myles Brown was born at Lower Brighton, six miles north of my home town of Woodstock. As a young man he took a course in bookkeeping, and worked for the Fraser Company at Plaster Rock. One day a New York sportsman—who had several times talked with Myles—and was attracted by his good humour and pleasing manner, suggested to the young man that he go to New York where he would get him a much better paying job.

In due course Myles went. His job was a good one and he rapidly rose from one position to another. Eventually he moved to Gates Mills, Ohio, and started a machine-tool factory, became a millionaire, fished and hunted all over Canada and Alaska, and had the largest private collection of game heads in North America.

This, then, was the Carleton County man who bid in the Pratt water put up for auction in 1952. I first met him on the Restigouche about twenty-five years ago. He was leaving the next day. As our canoes came in to the float he ran down the long flight of steps and said, "I'm Myles Brown," shook hands with us and then helped shoulder our dunnage and carry it up to The Lodge. He was wonderful!

* * *

Two Brooks Lodge is situated on a level bench some thirty feet above the river. Back of it the terrain rises in a wooded ridge; and from a boiling spring situated near the top of another high hill—almost a mountain—water is conveyed by a two-inch pipe almost a half-mile into The Lodge. Across the river, which at this point is only about one hundred feet wide, is a high promontory covered with evergreens, poplar, and beautiful white birches. It is an idyllic spot. Two hundred yards below The Lodge two ice-cold brooks—one on each side of the river—rush down deep gorges and give The Lodge its name.

I was invited to fish Myles's water every year after he acquired it, but was only able three times to avail myself of his generosity.

Myles had good guides and a cook who turned out the most delicious meals. One of his guides was Albert Goodine who, as I have said earlier, guided the celebrated Harry Chestnut on every salmon river in New

Brunswick, the Island of Anticosti, and on Newfoundland waters; and, after Mr. Chestnut passed on, guided on the Government Open Water on the Restigouche.

As I have said before, the salmon in the Upsalquitch are not large, though occasionally a big one runs up from the Restigouche. Perhaps it is an adventurer and likes to explore new waters. But the grilse—for some reason I cannot fathom—are much larger than those on the latter river, going to five pounds and, like the salmon, are splendid sport on light tackle. The scenery far surpasses that on the Restigouche. The season of 1958, the salmon were more plentiful than for many previous years. More than one angler took his limit—twenty fish in one week.

There were generally six rods present; each man being assigned the several pools in rotation, so that he had a chance to fish them all—generally twice during the week. It was always an exciting and anticipatory occasion when the canoes departed in the mornings; but it could not compare with the restrained excitement on their return at midday, and the end of the day. As each canoe swung in to the wooden float, and the angler got out, followed by his guide carrying his catch, those who had arrived earlier rose from their seats on the wide verandah to cluster at the head of the long flight of steps. In fancy I can yet hear Myles's hearty, "What luck?—Two—Good!"

Myles's wife, affectionately known as Millie, was there (she always accompanied him to the river) gracious, competent, kindly, a splendid hostess, she fitted into the scene and quietly glorified it. She was an ardent angler and often when she fished came in high rod at the end of the day. Two Brooks Lodge would not have been the same without Millie Brown!

The *Rock* Pool—above Boland Brook—is the last lower pool we fished. Above it is *Little Indian*, then *Big Indian*, then *Caribou*—the latter fronting a gentle moss-covered hillside and flat, once a favourite feeding ground for caribou. Above this, a half-mile, is *Two Rocks*, from which, in late August, a few minutes after dusk had fallen, I raised, hooked, and lost a fine fish.

The *Home Pool*, opposite The Lodge, is a good producer. From this Millie often brought in the "bacon". Above the Home Pool is *Monell's*, named after some long-ago angler. Then comes *Humbug*. Why *Humbug*? It is a good pool and most anglers like it. I fancy the name arose from the fact that some disappointed angler exclaimed: "It's a humbug!" Here I once hooked and lost five salmon in succession. What was wrong? Had I lost my art? Finally I reeled in and discovered that the barbs of my hook were broken off!... Then there is *Upper Rock Pool*; and *Long Look-um*—where for three quarters of a mile the river runs as straight as a crow can fly. We can imagine an Indian, many years ago, gazing up its long expanse and saying "It's a long look-um." The *Promontory Pool* gets its name from a flanking high wooded knoll. I like *The Promontory*. Usually the fish rest in shallow water on the right hand shore. I landed two salmon. Above *The Promontory* is *The Rapids*; then *The Popologan Pool*, the last on Myles's water.

What visions of success and failure, and withal what memories of jolly times these names conjure up. And to those who fish them in future years I give them the Anglers' Blessing—"Good Luck!"

* * *

Henry Widdell was a guest at Two Brooks Lodge when I was there in 1958. Hank was an ardent angler and at the end of the week was high rod. Naturally he was pleased. Immured in an office the greater part of the year, or making flights all over Europe, Canada, and the United States, he could not get enough of the out-of-doors. It was a daily ritual to have the cook pack lunch for him and his guide. Then, at noon hour, they went to shore and built a little fire, and boiled water for tea, or coffee, and fried steak, or it might be bacon and eggs. This noon-hour meal beside a fire was the highlight of the day for Hank. It was a renewal of his boyhood when he buried potatoes in a pile of burning autumn leaves and, although only half cooked, ate them with that relish which only youth knows.

Although a millionaire, there were no silly frills about Hank. He talked frankly and freely about his boyhood days and the struggle to get an education. One evening, as we were all seated about the table in the lodge dining-room, someone spoke about homemade bread; of how superior it was to the bakers' loaf. And Hank said: "I remember the big two-decker loaves my mother used to make. I can see them now, fresh from the oven, ranked on the kitchen table; the top crust a beautiful golden colour. And the smell—? I used to stand and inhale it as men coming from a coal pit do fresh air." Then, a faraway look in his eyes, "My mother would cut me a thick slice, spread butter over it, then a layer of brown sugar. It was ambrosia. Never since have I tasted anything to compare with it."

Such was Hank. We all liked him. He told me he would gladly give one thousand dollars if he could hook and land a twenty-five pound salmon.

I pity the man, or the woman, or the child, who has never sat beside an open fire in the house. For the flames, dancing up the chimney, glorify the room. An open fire is articulate with memories of a past when it was the only means of warmth and for cooking purposes. It was the altar about which the family gathered for devotions when family Bible-reading and prayers were considered as essential to man's life as eating and drinking.

I know of several such great fireplaces—with enormous cranes and hand-wrought iron fire-dogs—now, alas, boarded up. I was told that the cold air drafted down the chimney, and the wide open fireplace, and robbed the house of the heat generated by stove or furnace. But I think sadly of something more precious they have lost.

When we were married, my wife and I said we would have two things in our home: a fireplace, and a piano. Personally I would rather dispense with my dining-room table, and eat off a soapbox, than with my open fire. What a sense of comfort, of tranquillity, an open fire imparts on a winter day with the snow blowing like smoke across the fields, or from the roofs of nearby houses; and the wind whistling and keening along the eaves of my dwelling. Then a good book in my hands, or some writing to do; and my pipe going; and my wife doing a bit of mending, or her nose buried in a book—for she reads much.

* * *

Six Salmon Rivers and Another

And I pity those—especially children—who have never sat beside a little fire in the out-of-doors. I have seen the eyes, the faces of children, flooded with ecstasy at the kindling of a fire, the like of which our pagan ancestors venerated as a god. How the young folk love to gather the makings: the curly birch-bark that, no matter how old, still retains its magical, highly inflammable oil. I can see them flitting between the boles of the trees and picking up dry limbs that have fallen to earth, and breaking them in suitable lengths across their knees. Then, each with an armful, hastening to the circle of stones I had made to confine our fire so that it would not spread and burn the forest.

How quickly the oily birch-bark beneath the laid sticks steals the flame of the lighted match—as though it hungered for it—and curls and writhes, and gives off inky-black smoke, and yields up its life in intense heat which ignites the whole pile into a glorious blaze. And the children gather about, sitting, or on bended knees, their eyes cupping their adoration of this wondrous thing coaxed to life from a few pieces of wood and a roll of birch-bark. And then, when it begins to die down, they rise to their feet with one accord and scurry among the trees gathering more dry branches. No Persian convert of Phoedima[44] was ever more anxious to keep his fire-god burning than are these youngsters to revivify the flames of their woodland altar.

* * *

One evening, during my first trip to the Upsalquitch, I mentioned to Myles that I felt quite sure there must have been a prehistoric Indian campsite at The Forks, and that, if he didn't mind, I'd like to take my spade (I always carry one with me) and do some exploring the next day instead of fishing. "Do whatever you like," he said. "I'll tell your guide to take a lunch along, and you can stay all day."

---

44 Phoedima, widow of Smerdis, 521-485 BCE, was thought to have introduced fire-worship into Persia.

The Upsalquitch

The cook, well aware of my guide's capacity, packed a big container with food, and in the morning we set off. I think my guide was secretly disgusted; he wanted me to catch salmon.

We arrived at The Forks about eleven a.m. Selecting a spot near the river—where I could see both the Northwest Branch and the Southeast Branch—I immediately began digging a trench about six feet long by one in depth. Within less than ten minutes I unearthed a beautiful agate arrowhead of Micmac make. But the artificer who had so patiently chipped it had brought it with him on one of his hunts, for no such stones were found on the Upsalquitch.

Odd, how quickly news travels in the wilderness. Next day, which was Saturday, it was known at Miss Parsons' Lodge twelve miles distant—that I had found an arrowhead at The Forks. And on the following Tuesday, when my angling friend, Cecil Stewart, and I were going home by car, and stopped at the gate where all who travel to or from the woods must report to the caretaker and show their permits, she told me she had heard of my experience at The Forks.

But previously, on Sundays, Miss Parsons and two of her guests, Mr. and Mrs. Turnbull of New York, had come up the river to pay an informal visit to Mr. and Mrs. Brown. I was introduced, and soon the conversation turned on Indian artifacts. Miss Parsons told me there were several curious mounds on her property between The Lodge and Boland Brook, and she would be happy if I were to come down and do some excavating.

I did, but found no evidences of Indian occupation in the three or four mounds I dug into. But I'm quite positive Indians camped there. A level bit of ground especially caught my fancy but, as it was closed with a wire fence behind which was a bull (I do not like bulls) I decided not to attempt any digging on its preserve. It had done that in moments of anger.

Two months later I had a letter from Miss Parsons, then back in New York. Millie Brown had loaned her one of my books to read and she wanted to make some comments about it. She also told me that her cook, Mrs. William Ferguson, had been much disappointed that she hadn't seen me during my visit to The Lodge. She told Miss Parsons that her husband,

Six Salmon Rivers and Another

Bill, had guided me three years in succession on the Kedgwick. Needless to say I too was disappointed at not meeting Mrs. Ferguson, for twice—while passing through Woodstock—she had called at my office in the hope of seeing me, but on both occasions I was out of town.

* * *

Opportunities to do those things we much desire often have a habit of again presenting themselves, and only depend for their consummation by accepting them. The opportunity to meet Mrs. Ferguson occurred a year later while I was again at *Two Brooks Lodge*, and after fishing the upper pools, I had reached *The Rock Pool*, half a mile from Boland Brook and Miss Parsons' lodge. I had only made a few casts when I said to my guide: "To heck with fishing! I want to go downriver and call on Mrs. Ferguson."

"Oh!" he said, then reluctantly pulled up the kitty, fastened the rope, started his motor, and off we went.

The canoe reached shore. I got out, and walked up the path leading towards The Lodge and its adjoining buildings. On the way I met one of Miss Parsons' guides and stopped to speak to him. Thinking I had come to see her, he said that she was not arriving until the following day but all the help was present... Yes, Mrs. Ferguson was over there, pointing to a building to the right of The Lodge. I thanked him, went to the door and knocked. It was opened by a woman past middle age, of medium height, buxom, dressed in a spotless frock of some printed material. Her face was unlined, fair complexioned with kindly blue eyes; her hair, almost white, curled in natural waves over her finely shaped head. "Will you come in?" she asked. The room—it was the kitchen—was filled with the indescribable odour of recent cooking—my eyes lighted on a big bowl heaped with golden-brown doughnuts.

Remembering that during the winter evenings she had sat in her home kitchen reading my book to her own children and some of the neighbours; that twice she had called at my office to see me; that she was the wife of my old guide, I impulsively put one arm around her shoulder, and leaning forward kissed her on the cheek. Then I drew back.

There was a puzzled look in her eyes that said, plain as day: Doubtless I ought to remember you; especially since you have taken a liberty no stranger would think of, let alone put into effect in such a sanguine manner... Of course you must be an old friend. Then, to clear up the enigma, she spoke: "Just who might you be—anyway?"

I told her. She took my hand, shook it heartily, her face wreathed in a happy smile. "Oh," she said, "Doctor Clarke! Bill's—our Doctor Clarke! I've wanted to meet you for years."

She drew out a chair for me, then one for herself, and we sat down and talked; about Bill, her children, and grandchildren. Then she went into another room—adjoining the kitchen—and presently returned with a heap of photographs and snapshots. Again seating herself, she passed them to me one by one, explaining what child this was, what grandchild another. This one was Jack—"You remember he was with Bill, guiding, the last year you were on Kedgwick."

Thus the minutes glided on, both of us reminiscing on the past. Finally, she said: "Would you care for a doughnut and a cup of tea?"

Needless to say, I answered yes. So she took two of the circular brown doughnuts out of the big bowl, put them on a plate, brought them to me, then poured a cup of tea.

Never have I tasted such doughnuts. They were light, and flaky, and wholly delicious. I ate slowly to prolong my enjoyment.

At last I rose to go and we shook hands in farewell. Then she said: "Please wait a moment; I want you to have another doughnut—and one for your guide." So saying, she swept back to the bowl, and taking out two, wrapped them in a paper napkin and gave them to me.

A few rods from the house I paused, turned and looked back. She was standing on the doorstep, her sweet, kindly face smiling. A little wind stirred her wavy white hair, I lifted my hand in final farewell, and she lifted hers. I was inexpressibly happy, as I'm sure she had been pleased that I had taken the time to call on her. Memories had been renewed of an irreplaceable past when she had been a mother with growing children, and the loving wife of the man whose informing comradeship I had enjoyed on many a salmon pool. But, had it not been for the jasper arrowhead I found at The Forks, I might never have had the pleasure of meeting her.

I found my guide talking with two of Miss Parsons' help. I apologized for my long stay. He said that was all right; he'd had a good time.

So had I—an unforgettable hour. He ate his doughnut. Then I got into the canoe; he followed me and with his setting pole shoved it into deeper water, and started the motor; then we sped up the lovely river which, because of my late experience, had now become even more beautiful.

— CHAPTER X —

THE OTHER RIVER

As a child I was often disappointed when on certain days it rained and I could not go out to play, or to fish Marven's Brook, and would vent my discontent by using my only swear words: "Blame the luck!" Then my mother would say: "The sun is shining above the clouds. It will be a fair day tomorrow, or the next, or the day after. It has always been that way, and always will. So remember that God made this day as He did the others, and be contented." And when I desired something—it might be a new suit of clothes which she told me the state of the family finances would not then permit, and I retorted that young B.J. had recently got one, she quietly reminded me it was not the clothes that mattered, but what was in my head and heart; and went on to explain what she meant. Thus by these and many other examples of her wisdom, she tried to guide my bark along the river of contentment. She had never read—nor even heard of—Marcus Aurelius Antoninus, but, firmly believing in the order of things, she had learned "to bear with what universal nature brings."[45] And would have said with Cobbett: "Happiness or misery is in the mind."

* * *

---

45   Marcus Aurelius, *Meditations*.

To be contented with little. Epictetus, the crippled slave, says: "As it is better to be in good health, being hard pressed on a little truckle bed, than to roll and to be ill in some broad couch, so too is it better on a little competence to enjoy the calm of moderate desires, than in the midst of superfluities."[46]

But we desire so many things of lesser worth that the seeds of contentment often never take root, while the clock of time inexorably ticks out the last years of opportunity. Every man, whatsoever his circumstances, is equally poor who fails to realize not only the beauty, the goodness, the kindness, and the charity that surround us, but also that he may be "the master of his inner self." Walton, the father of anglers, possessed all these virtues and more. Of whose *Compleat Angler* Charles Lamb wrote to his friend Coleridge: "It breathes the very spirit of innocence, purity, and simplicity of heart.... It would sweeten a man's temper at any time to read it; it would Christianise every angry, discordant passion; pray make yourself acquainted with it."[47]

* * *

And so, remembering all these, although I cannot always retain that tranquillity of spirit which is the ideal of Nature, I can—to further paraphrase the words of Richard Jefferies—at least think of it and try to attain it.

THE END

---

[46] Epictetus, Greek Stoic philosopher, c. 55-135 CE, *Discourses*.

[47] *The Letters of Charles Lamb*.

INDEX

A

Allen, Colonel John 95
Artefacts, Maliseet . 14, 52, 96, 103, 108-9, 185

B

Baker, Harry 127
Barbauld, Anna Letitia
   poem "Life! I know not what thou art" . 122
Bartholomew's River 11
Bear, Noel, Indian hunter and trapper . . . 181
Beaverbrook, Lord (Max Aitken) 3
Becaguimec Stream 101
Bedding, Sam 104-5
Bedell Brook 11-13
Beechwood Dam 89, 107
Belyea, Dr 72
Betsy Rapids 96
Big Black Rapids 181
Big Clearwater 63-64, 76
Big Falls 11
Big Gulquac Stream 185
Big Indian (pool) 193
Big Push (pool) 73
Bill, a guide. . . . 12, 63-67, 73, 75-79, 81, 83
Birch Island 77
Black Dose, salmon fly 137, 153
Blake, W H.
   A Fisherman's Creed 16, 72, 80, 133
Boiestown, NB   7, 13, 51-52, 63-64, 66-67, 75, 80-82, 85
Boland Brook 191
Borrow, George. 116
Boyce's Rocks 52
Boyer, Russell. . 19, 21-22, 24-36, 109, 111-14, 116, 118-22, 132, 141
   cocktails; Matutinal cocktail, 113-14; Thunder an' lightning, 1 14; Vesper cocktail, 112-13, 120
   death 121
   and the Dryad. 114-21
   his island 1 10-11
   recites poetry 111, 119
   Russell's toast 121-22
   in story "The Way to Understanding" 19- 21, 23-32, 34-36
Brandy Brook 163
Brawn, Duffy. 1-2
Bristol, NB 102-3
Broderick, John, outfitter. 126
Broderick's fishing lodge 128, 136, 144-45, 161
Brown Fairy, salmon fly 56
Brown, Millie (Mrs. Myles Brown) . 193, 197
Brown, Myles 189, 191-94, 196
Browne, Sir Thomas 133
Burnt Hill Rapids 53-54, 64, 73
Burroughs, John, conservationist. 58
Butcher, salmon fly. 137

C

Cadillac, Antoine, sieur de Cadillac 88
Campbell, Steve, guide 152-53
Campbellton, NB 128, 146, 162, 189
Caribou, pool on Upsalquitch 193
Carleton County, NB 185, 192
Cartier, Jacques. 123
Cascapedia River 124
Chaleur, Baie de 123-24, 128, 146
Champlain, Samuel de 87-88, 133
Charlie, a guide. . 56-57, 62-63, 70, 76-77, 82
Chestnut, Harry 143, 155, 192
Cheyne, (a Scotsman) 126, 148, 151-52

Index

Cheyne, salmon pool 148, 151, 164
Clark, Charles (Charlie) . . 140, 144, 151, 161, 166, 183
Clarke, George Frederick
    childhood 1, 3-11; fights lubberly boy, 6-9; fishes in snow pools, ... 3
    Chris in Canada 136
    conservation 6; dams, 6, 86, 107, 147; Mactaquac dam, 91, 96; Tobique Narrows dam, ... 182
    digs for artefacts . . . 14, 96, 103, 108, 185
    grandfather spears salmon. 4-5
    poem "New faces come". 141
Clarke, Maria
    childhood; fishing, ... 5
    tells GFC about salmon. 9
Cobbett, William. 191
Cody, Rev. H.A.
    poem "Don't you hear them coming" . 71-72
Connecticut, River, U.S.A. 147
Cow Dung, salmon fly 137
Crooked Rapids 17, 189
Cruger, Lt-Colonel 98

D

Dashwood, Captain Richard 124, 190
    Chip-lo-quorgan, or Life by the Campfire . 123
de Chute, River. 11
de la Tour, Charles 88
De Lancey's Brigade 97
De Monts, Pierre. 87-88, 133
Dead Pool 186
Denys, Nicholas 58-59, 88
Department of Lands & Mines . 146, 148, 162
Devil's Elbow Rapids. 163
Devil's Half Acre (pool) 162-63
Diogenes 111
Down's Gulch Brook. 162

Drummond, Henry
    poem "The Devil and Daniel Webster" . 111
Dungarvon, tributary of Miramichi 11
Dungarvon Whooper (legend and lumberman's folk song) 67, 80
Dungeon, The (pool) 16-17

E

Eel River 95
Ek-pa-hawk, NB 96
Epictetus 202
Erikson, Leif 106

F

Fairfax, Janet and Ronald
    in story "The Way to Understanding" 19- 36
Fall Brook (Kedgwick) 140
Fall Brook (Miramichi) 76
Fenwick, Rev. L.A. 51
Ferguson, Bill (guide) . 128-32, 136, 138, 141, 198
Ferguson, Guy (guide) 140, 163
Ferguson, Mrs William 198-200
Ferguson's Tum. 189
Fifteen Mile Brook. 11
Flemming, Premier Hugh John 102
Forks of Cascapedia 124
Forks of Miramichi . . 13, 15-16, 22, 49-51, 85
Forks, of Miramichi 13
Forks of Upsalquitch . . 189, 191, 196-97, 200
Frank's Brook 11
Franquelin, Baptiste Louis 54, 57, 86
Fraser Company 142, 144, 192
Fraser Company (Montreal) 17

G

Galissoniere, Roland-Michel, Marquis . . 91
Gallant, Adelard, guide 151-52

Index

Gillalpen, Bill (guide) 57, 59-67
Glane, Mr 104
Glasier, John 71
Goodine, Albert (guide) . . 137, 155, 164, 192
Government Open Water . . 143, 151, 162-63, 165, 193
Grafton, NB 99
Grand Falls. 71, 90
Grant, Dr Nelson P. 15-17, 24, 37, 91, 139-40, 144, 151, 157, 183, 185-86
Grant, Levi. 17
Green River 127
Grog Island 163
Guimec Stream 101-2
Gulquac Lodge. 144, 183
Gulquac Pool. 186-87
Gulquac Stream, Big. 183
Gulquac Stream, Little. 183
Gyles, John. 96-97

H

Hailes, Archie 94
Half Moon Cove. 13, 51, 54
Hannah, Harley 49
Hardy salmon fishing rod 17, 184
Harper's New Monthly Magazine 127
Hartland, NB. . . . 91, 102, 110, 115, 117, 121
  longest covered bridge in the world . . . 102
Hartland Pool 101-2, 115, 117, 119
Hayes Bar 85
Hazlitt, William
  Table Talk 191
Hell's Gate 163
Henry, guide and cook 57-58, 60-62, 68, 70-71, 76-77, 85
Hilda's Rock 165-66
Holmes, Oliver Wendell 108
Home Brew Song (lumberman's folk song) . . 80

Home Pool. 194
Houlton, Maine, U.S.A. 6
Hudson, River, U.S.A. 147
Humbug Pool 194

I

Indian Lookout 92, 95
Irving, Washington
  story "Rip Van Winkle" 75

J

Jefferies, Richard
  The Life of the Fields 121, 202
Jock Scott, salmon fly 21, 137-39
Joe Jefferson's Rock. 75
Johnson, Samuel 135
Juniper, NB. 57

K

Karlsefni 106
Kedgwick River 24, 126-31, 136, 139, 141-42, 144, 146, 148, 152, 163, 198-99
  Quata-wam-Kedgewick. 124
Kennedy, Bill 144, 151, 158-60, 183-86
Kipling, Rudyard 111

L

La Farge, Mr and Mrs 126
La Plante, Josephine 158-59
Larry (author's Indian guide, and friend)17- 18, 21, 24-25, 37, 55, 57, 62, 67, 72-73, 76, 82, 85
Larry 's Pool 158, 164
Little Black Rapids. 181
Little Cross Point Island 162, 165
Little Gulquac pool 183
Little Indian Pool 193
Little Main Restigouche 126

205

Index

Little Push (pool) 73
Little Southwest Miramichi 181
Little Tobique River 190
Long Look-Um Pool 194
Louey Falls or Rapids 52
Lumberman's Alphabet (lumberman's folk song)
. . . . .70, 79

M

MacCormack, Angus. 13-14
Mack, R.T., outfitters. 184
MacKenzie, Murdoch, guide and outfitter . 13, 16-17
Mactaquac dam . . . 89, 91, 96, 102, 107, 118
Magnus, Olaus 134
Maliseet, NB 181-82
Maliseets (St John River Indians) 56, 72, 95-96, 99 102, 108, 127, 134, 181, 189
Mar Lodge, salmon fly 137
Marcus Aurelius Antoninus 201
Marlowe, Christopher
  Tamburlaine the Great 154
Marston, Perley. 139
Marven's Brook. 201
Matapedia River 124
McGivney Junction 85
McKeel Brook 52
McNair, Marian 147
Medoctec, ancient village of Maliseet Indians 89, 95, 97
Meduxnekeag, River 1, 6, 8, 97
Micmac Club. 139
Micmac Indian tribe . 56, 58-59, 123, 130, 134, 189
Millionaire's Pool. 163
Miramichi Fire (folk song) 71, 79
Miramichi, Little Southwest 181

Miramichi River . 12, 17, 54-55, 67-68, 74-75, 83, 103, 142, 189
  Main Northwest. 181
  Main Southwest. . 4, 11, 13, 15, 51, 53, 128
  North Branch 17
  South Branch 18
Monell's Pool. 194
Moulton, Noel 108, 163
  story "my great-great-great-great-great-grandfather". 109
Moulton, Tom 181-82
Mul-qua-pun (Indian bread) 61
Murray, Allie, guide . . . 144-45, 161-62, 164

N

Nackawick stream 91-93
Nagoot (Tobique) 181
Narrows, The (Tobique) 182
Nictau Lake 181, 190
Nigger Rafting Ground (pool) 163
Nighthawk, salmon fly 21, 129, 137
Nixon, Joe 50
No. 5 Pool 164
No. 7 Pool 164
No. 8 Pool 164
No Man's Island Northeast Carry 181

O

O'Neil, Jerry 93
O'Rourke, Terrence. 104-6
Ogilvy, David, guide and outfitter 144-45, 147, 156, 159-60, 162, 183, 185
Ogilvy, Hendry, guide and outfitter . 144, 159, 184, 186
Ogilvy, John (Jock), guide and outfitter . .144, 147, 162, 165, 183, 185
Olaus Magnus 134
Old Hen and Chickens, The, rocks. 52

Index

P

Palmer, Jim 104, 106
Pancost Pool 159, 164-66
Parmachene-belle, trout and salmon fly 28
Parsons, Miss K. De B., outfitter 189, 191, 197-98, 200
Patterson Pool 99
Peelhead (lumberman's folk song). 80
Penman (Charles Hallock)
  "The Restigouche" 123, 125-27, 129-30, 148, 163, 189
Penobscot River 89
  dam 147
Perry, Joe 92
Peter Emberley (lumberman's folk song) .68, 79
Pilot Pond 76
Piscator (character in *The Compleat Angler*) 62, 150-51
Popologan
  Brook 191
  Pool 194
Priest's Rock, The, pool. 183
Promontory Pool, The 194
Push-An'-Be-Damned Rapids. . 52, 55, 63-65

R

The Rapids pool 194
Renous River. 11
Restigouche River . . .123-26, 141-47, 151, 155, 163, 165, 181, 184, 187, 189-90, 192
Restigouche Salmon Club 146, 162
Reversing Falls, St John River 87
Riparian Association 145-46, 162
Rock Pool 193, 198
Rocky Bend Rapids 76
Rod and Gun Magazine. 132, 136
Run, The, pool 120, 148, 151-52, 164

Russell, Jack, outfitter 143

S

Saint Croix, River 124
Saint John, NB 71, 124
Saint John River 6, 11, 87-89, 91-93, 97, 101-2, 105, 110, 112, 120-21, 132, 181-82
Salmon
  smoked/smoking 6, 156-57
  spearing 5-6, 60, 99, 125
Salmon Hole (pool) . 16-17, 21-22, 49-50, 85, 110
Schoodic lakes 124
Service, Robert W., poem "The Cremation of Sam McGee" 111, 132
Sevogle Stream 190
Shiktahawk River 102, 104
Silver Doctor, salmon fly . .21, 92, 100, 137-38
Sisters Brook 11
Slate Island 52, 55-56
Slate Island Brook 59
Smith, Captain Jacob 97-98
Smith, Judith 99
Smith, Richard 98
Soldier's Pool 126
Soldier's Run 143-44
Soloutre, France
  blades 103
Stewart, Cecil 197
Stillwater Pool 162
Stories
  Bill and Silas sing to bullfrogs. 77-81
  digging for gold: the golden calf. . . .95-96
  digging for gold: tomcats 92-95
  digging for gold: Vikings 103-6
  Horace the stuffed bear 63-67
  Noel Moulton; "my great-great-great-great-great-grandfather", ... 109

Index

    painting a salmon fly 100
    The Way to Understanding 19-37
Sullivan, Joe 166

T

Taxis River 85
Teed, E.R. 127
Temperance Shoals. 163
Thoreau, Henry David 89, 111, 135
    Maine Woods, The 89
Three Mile Rapids 52, 76
Tobique River 11, 91, 107, 142, 144, 147, 181-83, 185-86, 189
Tracy Brook 162
Trotting Ground (pool) 162
Trout Brook Pond 77
Trowser's Lake 181, 183
Two Brooks Lodge 192-94, 198
Two Mile Pool 129
Two Rocks Pool 193

U

Upper Five Mile Pool 140
Upper Rock Pool 194
Upper Two Mile Pool 128
Upsalquitch, River . .161, 181, 189-91, 193-98

V

Vaudreuil, Pierre, Marquis de Vaudreuil . . .91
Victoria Corner, NB 110-12, 119
Vimy Ridge World War I battlefield . . 60, 104, 106

W

Waagan. 126
Waagansis 126
Walton, Izaak. 151
    The Compleat Angler . 4, 13, 51, 55, 150, 154, 202
Waps-ke-heg-an, or Wapske
    Flat .108
    River. 11
West Brook. 11
White Water Brook 134, 139-40
Widdell, Henry 194-95
Wilkinson (salmon fly). 137
William Q.
    story of golden calf 95-96
Woodstock, NB 1, 4, 6, 98-100
Wyers Pool. 140

www.ingramcontent.com/pod-product-compliance
Lightning Source LLC
Chambersburg PA
CBHW021123300426
44113CB00006B/268